"This inspiring and eminently readable bo[...] Christian interpreter, provides a lucid intr[...] God-centered thought. Written with earn[...] *Approaching God* demonstrates how Hesch[...] Judaism can favor theological humility, rel[...]"

> —Edward K. [...]
> Kaiserman [...]
> Author of *Spiritual Radical:*
> *Abraham Joshua Heschel in America*

"John Merkle has pondered the thought of Rabbi Abraham Joshua Heschel for many years. In *Approaching God*, Merkle provides readers with a discerning analysis of the wisdom of this eminent religious figure. Those who follow Merkle's sensitive exploration of Heschel will partake of this wisdom themselves."

> —Mary C. Boys, S.N.J.M.
> Skinner and McAlpin Professor of Practical Theology,
> Union Theological Seminary
> Author of *Has God Only One Blessing?*
> *Judaism as a Source of Christian Self-Understanding*

"John Merkle has produced a first-class study of the life and writings of Abraham Joshua Heschel, a man who has deeply influenced today's generation of theologians. Merkle has engaged thoughtfully with Heschel's approach to the divine-human encounter and *Approaching God* will be welcomed by Jews and Christians alike. Readers of this work are extremely fortunate to benefit from the author's lifelong interest in Heschel. The book not only provides an insight into this hugely significant Jewish theologian but also offers profound wisdom on the spiritual journey, daily undertaken by each and everyone of us."

> —Edward Kessler
> Executive Director, Woolf Institute of Abrahamic Faiths,
> Cambridge, England
> Author of *What Do Jews Believe?*

"Here is a lucid, powerful, and beautiful guide to one of the most compelling theologians of our time. If you do not know Heschel, prepare to be amazed and uplifted. If you do know Heschel, you will find in these pages even more to 'surprise the soul' and to delight the seeking heart."

> —David J. Wolpe
> Rabbi of Sinai Temple, Los Angeles
> Author of *Why Faith Matters*

APPROACHING GOD

THE WAY OF ABRAHAM JOSHUA HESCHEL

John C. Merkle

A Michael Glazier Book

LITURGICAL PRESS
Collegeville, Minnesota

www.litpress.org

A Michael Glazier Book published by Liturgical Press

Cover design by Ann Blattner

1   2   3   4   5   6   7   8   9

Library of Congress Cataloging-in-Publication Data

Merkle, John C.
    Approaching God : the way of Abraham Joshua Heschel / John C. Merkle.
      p.   cm.
    "A Michael Glazier book."
    Includes bibliographical references and index.
    ISBN 978-0-8146-5456-9 (pbk. : alk. paper)
    1. God (Judaism)   2. Heschel, Abraham Joshua, 1907–1972—Views on God.
  I. Title.

BM610.M47 2009
296.3092—dc22   2008051002

To

Harold Kasimow,

enlightened student of Heschel;

enlightening teacher of Heschel's thought,
of Judaism, and of other religions;

extraordinary contributor to interfaith dialogue
and understanding;

esteemed and cherished friend.

Contents

PREFACE

By giving this book the title and the subtitle it has, I mean to suggest that it explores both how Abraham Joshua Heschel perceives God relating to the world (God as an approaching God) and how he himself thinks about and responds to God (how he approaches God).

By suggesting that God is an approaching God, Heschel does not mean to imply that God is coming toward us because of being away from us. No, for Heschel, God is always present to us. But because we are not always present to God, Heschel suggests that God must "reach out" to us (from around us and from within us) to elicit our presence, our responsiveness. We dwell within the sphere of God's presence, yet God must strive to get us to appreciate that presence. God dwells within us, yet God must awaken us to the divine indwelling.

Heschel represents the best of monotheistic understanding when he claims that God's being "transcends mysteriously all conceivable being."[1] This means, among other things, that God's presence transcends all other types of presence. Though incomparably intimate, God's presence is, so to speak, "incognito" in ways unlike any other. Consequently, we must "search for God," strive to "find God," even though God is closer to us, more present within us, than we could ever begin to imagine.

We approach this ever-present (and yet in some sense unapproachable) divine reality by thinking about God, by trying to discern God's transcendent presence, and by striving "to live in a way that is worthy of that presence."[2] I can think of no better guide for our efforts at approaching God than Rabbi Heschel, whose thinking about God is replete with the most creative and provocative of theological insights, whose writings are evocative of God's presence in ways that challenge us to strive to live in harmony with that presence.

The main purpose of this book is to explore Heschel's insights about God in the hope that they might help readers in their own approaches to God. But before engaging in a sustained exposition and analysis of Heschel's theological insights, I begin with an introduction, "Heschel's Witness to God," that offers a brief overview of Heschel's life and works in the service of God. There was real harmony between Heschel's way of living and his way of thinking, and I offer this biographical introduction in the hope that readers will find that harmony just as inspirational for their own ways of approaching God as they will find the insights explored beyond the introduction.

Chapter 1, "Nature, Humanity, and God," explores Heschel's insights about how human experiences of nature and humanity convey the reality and presence of God and constitute grounds for faith in God. This kind of exploration is often referred to as "natural theology," focusing on what is called the "general revelation" of God through nature, including human nature and existence, as distinct from God's "special revelation" attested to in the Bible. Heschel's approach to this special revelation is the subject of the second chapter, "God's Revelation to the Jewish People." This is followed in chapter 3, "Jewish Responses to God," with a discussion of what in many of his writings Heschel elucidates as the principal components of Jewish religious life: worship, learning, and ethical action. Chapter 4, "God and Religious Diversity," then explains how Heschel, unwavering in his commitment to one particular religion, sees diversity of religions as the will of God.

It is now more than two decades since the publication of my book *The Genesis of Faith: The Depth Theology of Abraham Joshua Heschel* (Macmillan, 1985). Since then a number of colleagues and friends have urged me to publish an abridged and more accessible version of that book, filled as it is with lengthy philosophical arguments and explanatory endnotes. Grateful for their encouragement, I have decided to write this new book in the hope of introducing Heschel's approach to God to a wider audience than I have reached through *The Genesis of Faith*. While this book is very different than would be an abridged version of that earlier work, it incorporates in revised form some material from it.

In my view, Heschel was the most creative and insightful American religious thinker of the twentieth century. I know of no author from any religious tradition who has written more eloquently than he about the reality and presence of God. Heschel's prose is highly poetic and reads like outbursts of insight woven together into evocative paragraphs and chapters. Because of this, many of his readers find it difficult to perceive any sustained philosophical or theological arguments in his writings. But I am convinced that these arguments are there amidst the inspired and inspiring pages—even if they are not cast in typical academic fashion. In this book I attempt to explicate, in a manner accessible not only to professional philosophers and theologians, the logic and coherence of Heschel's approach to God and to show that it contains cogent arguments for (1) affirming the reality and presence of God; (2) believing in God's revelation as attested to in the Bible; (3) the importance of responding to God by way of worship, learning, and ethical action; and (4) accepting religious diversity as the will of God.

Having taught a college course titled "The Reality of God" for many semesters, I am convinced that college students should be introduced to and challenged by Heschel's way of thinking about and responding to God. I hope this book will encourage students to make Heschel one of their spiritual guides for years to come, and that through him they will grow in an appreciation of what the Jewish tradition has to offer all of us, whether Jewish or not, about the abiding significance of God in our lives.

Acknowledgments

First and foremost, I am deeply grateful to my beloved spouse, Sarah Pruett, whose loving presence in my life has immeasurably enhanced my appreciation of what Heschel means by God's presence in our lives. Although her immense learning and her wisdom have been nourished primarily by sources outside the field of theology, Sarah has consistently challenged and inspired my theological explorations. The astute questions and insights she shared in our conversations about the content of this book were invaluable to me as I wrote it, as also were her careful reading of the manuscript and her perceptive responses to it.

I am also deeply grateful to all those at the College of Saint Benedict and Saint John's University, especially to Rita Knuesel, the provost of these partner institutions, who made possible the recent sabbatical leave during which I wrote this book. Rita has been an ideal faculty colleague, dean, and provost, and the pleasure I have known at CSB/SJU during my thirty-two years there has been greatly enhanced by her support, inspiration, and friendship.

I also want to acknowledge with gratitude my first mentor in the study of Heschel, Professor Benjamin Willaert of Katholieke Universiteit Leuven, Belgium, who by his example convinced me that good reading and good conversation are more important than writing books. Probably the best-read person and most creative thinker I have ever met, he has rarely taken time away from reading, thinking, and conversing to publish his profound and provocative thoughts that made studying with him such a thrilling intellectual adventure. I would like to think that this book is worth even a fraction of a conversation or a class with Professor Willaert. Although it has been many years since I studied with him at Leuven, his inspiration endures.

Of the many scholars who have written books and essays about Heschel's life and thought, I am most indebted to Harold Kasimow. For three decades I have enjoyed being in regular dialogue with Harold, whose vast knowledge and keen insights have been invaluable for my own understanding of Heschel, of Judaism, and of other religions. Harold is a dear and generous friend, and I congratulate him for an illustrious career, from which he has recently retired, as a professor at Grinnell College in Iowa, where he was the George Drake Professor of Religious Studies. To him I am pleased to dedicate this book.

Heschel's Witness to God

"Here was a man for whom God was real," said renowned Protestant theologian Robert McAfee Brown about Abraham Joshua Heschel. "It is not very often these days that one finds a person who communicates this reality, not even among theologians."[1] Heschel communicated this reality of God through both words and deeds. After his death on December 23, 1972, one of his students was moved to say: "It was the love of God that was personified in him. The harp of this *zaddik's* [righteous person's] heart played day and night the echo of God's message."[2] Another scholar referred to Heschel's books as "the domain of written love, of a love that weaves sentences to celebrate God."[3] The chapters of this book explore major themes in Heschel's writings about God and the divine-human encounter. This introduction focuses briefly on Heschel's life and works in the service of God.

Childhood and Youth in Poland

Born in Warsaw in 1907, Abraham Joshua Heschel was the descendant, on both paternal and maternal sides of his family, of long lines of rabbis and scholars within a Jewish mystical movement known as Hasidism. Forged in Eastern Europe during the eighteenth century in response to the teaching of Reb Israel ben Eliezer (c. 1690–1760), known as the Baal Shem Tov (Master of the Good Name), Hasidism emphasizes the presence of God in daily life, and joy as a way of experiencing God.

Heschel grew up in an atmosphere of genuine Hasidic piety and learning, nurtured by a great wealth of Hasidic traditions and tales. In the introduction to his last book, *A Passion for Truth*, Heschel writes: "The earliest fascination I can recall is associated with the Baal Shem, whose parables disclosed some of the first insights I gained as a child."[4] But Heschel was also profoundly influenced by the only Hasidic leader to challenge some of the Baal Shem's principal teachings: Reb Menahem Mendl of Kotzk (1787–1859), known as the Kotzker Rebbe. (A rebbe is a Hasidic leader whose position is based on heredity or charisma.) In many ways, the Kotzker was the antithesis of the Baal Shem, and their dual influence upon the young Heschel perhaps accounts for much of the polarity and paradox in Heschel's later writings. The Baal Shem found God everywhere and rejoiced in God's presence. The Kotzker was dreadfully aware of God's absence and stormed the heavens, accosting God for permitting evil to exist in the world. The Baal Shem inspired joy and ecstasy, the Kotzker, fear and trembling.

Reflecting upon the influence of both the Baal Shem and the Kotzker on his life, Heschel writes: "I was taught about inexhaustible mines of meaning by the Baal Shem; from the Kotzker I learned to detect immense mountains of absurdity standing in the way. The one taught me song, the other—silence. The one reminded me there could be a Heaven on earth; the other shocked me into discovering Hell in the alleged Heavenly places in our world."[5]

"I must admit," says Heschel, "that during my entire life I struggled between being a hasid of the way of the Baal Shem or the way of the Kotzker Rebbe."[6] Perhaps combining the spirits of two such divergent masters in his own spirit largely accounts for the depth and breadth of insights found in Heschel's writings. Perhaps it was because Heschel never allowed either the Baal Shem or the Kotzker to prevail one over the other as his guide that Heschel's depictions of human existence and Jewish faith are so penetrating and complete. In an interview about fourteen months before his death, Heschel expressed his belief that the principle of polarity is essential to Judaism and he revealed that he consciously decided that it was his task "to find some kind of calculus by which to establish a polarity of the Kotzker and the Baal Shem—or of Judaism altogether."[7]

While Heschel's religious imagination and sensitivity were nurtured by tales and teachings of Hasidic masters, most of his youthful years were devoted to classical Jewish learning, the study of Bible and Talmud (the Mishnah, the first comprehensive postbiblical book of Jewish law, formulated about 200 CE, plus commentaries on the Mishnah, compiled from the third to the seventh centuries), and to study of the medieval Jewish mystical tradition known as Kabbalah. But Heschel achieved in his youth not only "*knowledge* of the Jewish religious heritage" but, as

Fritz A. Rothschild tells us, also "*understanding* for the realness of the spirit and for the holy dimension of all existence," which "was not primarily the result of book learning but the cumulative effect of life lived among people who 'were sure that everything hinted at something transcendent'; that the presence of God was a daily experience and the sanctification of life a daily task."[8]

But even if book learning was not the primary source of his religious understanding, nevertheless "by age thirteen, Heschel mastered the texts qualifying him to become a practicing rabbi," his biographer Edward K. Kaplan reports.[9] Advised to wait until he achieved even greater mastery of rabbinic sources, "Heschel was about sixteen years old when he was ordained" by one of his teachers, a prominent member of the Warsaw Rabbinical Council.[10] But the teenage rabbi longed for a secular education to complement his religious one, and to that end at age eighteen he moved to Vilna where for two years he matriculated at a modern Yiddish academy, broadening his education and developing his literary skills in preparation for university studies.

Studying, Writing, and Teaching in Germany

In April 1928 Heschel enrolled in the University of Berlin, where he earned his doctorate in philosophy in 1935. His doctoral dissertation on prophetic consciousness, published as *Die Prophetie* (On Prophecy) in 1936, forms the basis of the latter part of his monumental book *The Prophets*, published in 1962. The main themes of Heschel's dissertation and of his later book on the prophets are divine pathos—God's being affected by human beings even to the point of suffering—and human sympathy for and identification with divine pathos.

The religious philosophy that Heschel would develop throughout his lifetime began to take shape in his dissertation. The title of his major work of religious philosophy, *God in Search of Man*, published in 1955, expresses what Heschel considered to be the most fundamental insight of prophetic and rabbinic Judaism, that God takes the initiative in the divine-human relationship, reflecting God's loving concern for human beings. By basing his philosophy on the experience of God's concern, and on the insight that this concern means that God is moved by the plight and the deeds of human beings, "Heschel has propounded a truly revolutionary doctrine, challenging the whole venerable tradition of Jewish and Christian metaphysical theology."[11] God, as the Supreme Subject in search of human beings, as One who is compassionate toward them, affected by them, is not "the Unmoved Mover" of classical metaphysical theology, but is, in Fritz Rothschild's apt expression, "the Most Moved Mover" of biblical consciousness.[12] It is this consciousness of God that forms the foundation of Heschel's religious thought, and it is the explication of this consciousness that Heschel regarded as the "major effort" of his lifework.[13]

While Heschel's philosophical argument for the pathos of God challenges the tradition of classical metaphysical theology, as Rothschild rightly claims, it is not meant to challenge traditional Jewish understandings of God. To the contrary, as Heschel's daughter, Susannah Heschel, points out: "My father bases his understanding of divine pathos on a long, deep tradition within Judaism, most prominent in kabbalistic and Hasidic writings, but also found in the heart of rabbinic Judaism."[14]

Heschel was convinced that biblical and postbiblical Jewish references to God being affected by creatures, even to the point of suffering with them, make more theological or metaphysical sense than the standard claim of classical Greek-inspired metaphysical theology that God is unmoved by the plight of creatures. Heschel's philosophical theology, unlike classical metaphysical theology, was born not of abstraction from human experience but of an analysis of it, particularly an analysis of the experience of the biblical prophets and pious Jews down through the ages. A remote and apathetic God would have struck them "with a sense, not of dignity and grandeur, but rather of poverty and emptiness."[15]

While pursuing doctoral studies and writing his dissertation in German, Heschel also somehow found time to write poetry in his native Yiddish, and the major themes that he would work out philosophically are poignantly expressed in some of his earliest poems, such as "God Follows Me Everywhere" and "I and You," both published in 1929. The former clearly anticipates *God in Search of Man,* and the latter is obviously, though implicitly, an answer to Martin Buber's famous book *I and Thou,* published six years earlier, in which the human "I" seeks and dialogues with the divine "Thou." In three of the five stanzas, including the first stanza, of Heschel's "I and You," God is the "I." And God's relationship to the human "You" is not merely a matter of dialogue but of indwelling—and pathos: "I live in Me and in you. / Through your lips goes a word from Me to Me, / from your eyes drips a tear—its source in Me." The human response is full of sympathy for the God who dwells within: "When a need pains You, alarm me! / When You miss a human being tear open my door! / You live in Yourself, You live in me."[16] Here, in these lines, is the preeminent philosopher-poet of divine-human communion, sharing an intimacy he knew and an insight he cultivated from his War-saw days before the dawning of this poem until his death in New York some forty-three years after its publication. Here in these two poems is the prophetic mystic who from his earliest years through his last knew that God longs for the attention of those—all of us—in whom God lives.

But, for Heschel, more than God longs for the attention of human beings, God wants human beings to attend to each other. This theme, recurrent in many of Heschel's Yiddish poems, is expressed boldly in these lines of one titled "God and Man": "Not for Your own sake do You want sacrificial gifts; / only for those disappointed in Your love. / . . . Blasphemy pains You less / than people's despair. / He who blasphemes people, the world— / shames You, Almighty; / He who loves people— / brings joy to You, Holy One."[17]

The three poems here quoted are among sixty-six that constitute Heschel's first book, *Der Shem Hameforash: Mentsh* (The Ineffable Name of God: Man), published in 1933 while he was in the final stages of writing his doctoral dissertation. Throughout his life, Heschel was both a scholar and a poet. Most of his scholarly works are cast in a poetic prose that signifies the inseparability, at least for him, of theology and intense spiritual feeling. That the publication of his book of poems occurred during the time of his doctoral studies signaled what was to come: schol-arly works as things of beauty—and of soul.

While attending the university, Heschel also studied at Berlin's Hochschule für die Wissenschaft des Judentums (Academy of Scientific Jewish Scholarship), a seminary of Germany's Liberal Judaism, where he received a second rabbinic ordination in 1934. Thus, he not only was complementing his religious learning with a secular education; he also was complementing his traditional Hasidic education with a modern, historical-critical approach to Judaism. This undoubtedly helped Heschel enrich and broaden his already profound understanding of Judaism, and it prepared him well to communicate effectively throughout his life with different segments of the Jewish community. "Though himself eschewing labels, identifying wholly with none of these schools [in the world of Judaism], and all the while holding his own views, Heschel established good relations with each of the factions, since he believed each repre-sented, in greater or lesser measure, an affirmation of Jewish life. Heschel's breadth expressed the quality of his *'ahavat yisra'el* (love of Israel)."[18]

In 1934 Heschel assumed his first teaching position as an instructor in Talmud at the Berlin Hochschule from which he had just graduated.

In 1935 the publication of his biography of the Maimonides (1135–1204), the greatest of medieval Jewish scholars, "established his reputation as a fine scholar, a gifted and imaginative writer, and a master of German prose."[19] "Heschel's vivid life of the Rambam (as Maimonides is also known) spoke to Jews who had to live in Nazi Germany deprived of their religious culture" as he conveyed Maimonides' goal "to make his God-consciousness available to everyone, to sanctify the everyday."[20] In 1936 Heschel published a series of articles under the general title "Personalities of Jewish History" in a popular Berlin Jewish newspaper. Later described as acts of "spiritual resistance to the Nazis," these biographical sketches were designed to implicitly address "the situation of Jews in Germany" and to "hearten readers with a sense of divine purpose."[21]

Continuing his attempt to uplift German Jews through biographical writing in a time of extreme crisis, the next year Heschel published a short book on the great Portuguese Jewish philosopher Don Isaac Abravanel (1437–1509) to commemorate the five-hundredth anniversary of his birth. Heschel was convinced that emulating the loyalty to God displayed by Abravanel could strengthen German Jews who experienced persecution and faced exile not unlike the Portuguese and Spanish Jews of the late fifteenth century. "Abravanel's destiny offered a timeless guide to the present, as stated by the author's [Heschel's] italicized editorial comment: *'The Jewish question is a question of God to us.'*"[22]

Early in 1937, the same year his biography of Abravanel appeared, Heschel accepted the invitation of Martin Buber (1878–1965), Europe's most famous Jewish philosopher, to join the faculty of the Judische Lehrhaus, founded by another renowned Jewish philosopher, Franz Rosenzweig (1886–1929), in Frankfurt-am-Main. There Heschel led seminars, directed education activities, and gave public lectures until late October 1938, when he was deported by the Nazis. "During the nineteen months he lived in Frankfurt, Heschel announced his theology of history—and became the witness to the living God he remained throughout his life."[23]

Heschel was one of thousands of Polish Jews being sent back to their native country. But when the trains carrying them reached the border, Polish authorities refused to let them proceed home. After several days in a detention camp, Heschel was permitted to return to Warsaw where, within a few weeks of his arrival, he was hired as a substitute teacher of Bible and Jewish philosophy at the Warsaw Institute of Jewish Science for the remainder of the academic year. In April 1939 he received a life-saving invitation to join the faculty of Hebrew Union College in Cincinnati, Ohio. Three months later, just six weeks before the Nazi invasion of Poland, Heschel left Warsaw for London, where he would spend nearly a year before assuming his new academic post in the United States.

Life and Work in the United States

Heschel never forgot the horror of his last months in Germany and Poland. Twenty-five years later, upon assuming the Harry Emerson Fosdick Visiting Professorship at Union Theological Seminary in New York, he referred to himself as "a brand plucked from the fire of an altar of Satan on which millions of human lives were exterminated to evil's greater glory, and on which so much else was consumed: the divine image of so many human beings, many people's faith in the God of justice and compassion, and much of the secret and power of attachment to the Bible bred and cherished in the hearts of men for nearly two thousand years."[24] He was thirty-three years of age when he came to the United States, where lived for almost another thirty-three years until his death in 1972. During this second half of his life—as he consistently inspired reverence for the Bible, defended the divine image of all human beings, and fostered faith in the God of justice and compassion—he became for many what the great Reinhold Niebuhr called him: "the most authentic prophet of religious life in our culture."[25]

From 1940 until 1945 Heschel taught Jewish philosophy and rabbinics at Hebrew Union College. While there he continued the study of medieval Jewish philosophers that he had begun in Berlin, and he wrote his first book in English, *The Quest for Certainty in Saadia's Philosophy*. Published in 1944, this work is a penetrating study of the major questions—the meaning of truth, the sources of religious knowledge, revelation and reason, doubt and faith—explored by the father of medieval Jewish philosophy. Heschel continued to grapple with these questions throughout the course of his life and offered his own distinctive replies. What he said of Saadia Gaon may be said of Heschel himself: "He penetrated below the deep mines of Bible and Talmud, where he had unearthed a wealth of wisdom and learning in order to ascertain what lay in the substratum."[26]

Heschel remained forever grateful to those at Hebrew Union College who had secured his exodus from Poland, but while there he became increasingly aware of the disharmony between his approach to Judaism and the mission of the college. So in 1945, the same year he became a citizen of the United States, Heschel resigned his position at Hebrew

Union and joined the faculty at Jewish Theological Seminary of America in New York, where he subsequently became professor of Jewish ethics and mysticism and taught until the time of his death in 1972.

In 1946 Heschel married Sylvia Straus, a gifted pianist from Cleveland, Ohio, whom he had met while teaching in Cincinnati. Perhaps it was his marriage to a musician that moved Heschel, whose own speaking and writing had a melodious quality, to make the following observation: "The shattering experience of music has been a challenge to my thinking on ultimate issues. . . . Music leads to the threshold of repentance, of unbearable realization of our own vanity and frailty and of the terrible relevance of God. I would define myself as a person who has been smitten by music."[27] Together with their one daughter, Susannah, the Heschels made their home on Riverside Drive, several blocks from the seminary where he taught.

During his tenure at Jewish Theological Seminary, Heschel lectured widely throughout the United States and beyond, and he served as a visiting professor at several universities. During the 1965–66 academic year he was the first Jewish theologian to hold a visiting professorship at Union Theological Seminary in New York, located just across the street from Jewish Theological Seminary. At Union, Heschel drew more students to his classes than any other visiting professor in the school's history. But it was not only the students who came to him; he also reached out to them. According to J. A. Sanders, a prominent professor at Union, "Heschel made himself available to students and colleagues in ways that put the rest of the faculty to shame. Like the God of whom he spoke so warmly, Heschel was always there."[28]

All the while he was teaching, Heschel also continued to be a prolific writer, and his writings became widely read, even outside academic circles. "Every new book by Heschel intrigued Jews searching for roads back toward Judaism," writes Moshe Starkman. "More than anyone else in our time, he helped the seeking Jews gain vision to see the *maor sheb'yahadut*, the bright and brilliant within Judaism."[29]

But the influence of Heschel's books extends far beyond his Jewish audience. Explaining why Heschel's books and essays became "the devotional reading of myriads of non-Jews," renowned biblical scholar W. D. Davies writes: "Through his faith in the God beyond all mystery he ministered to our ultimate human need and, therefore, to us all. In his books and speeches, in which the cadences and rhythms and patterns of ancient synagogal prayers and sermons reverberate, . . . he called into being the emotions which he described, and summoned, not only Jews, but non-Jews also, to the depth of awe, wonder and mystery that life should evoke in [us] all."[30]

Heschel's most influential books written after World War II are the ones he wrote in English: *The Earth Is the Lord's: The Inner World of the Jew in East Europe* (1950), an eloquent tribute to the people from whom Heschel learned to develop his own inner world as a Jew; *The Sabbath: Its Meaning for Modern Man* (1951), a penetrating study of sanctity of time; *Man Is Not Alone: A Philosophy of Religion* (1951) and *God In Search of Man: A Philosophy of Judaism* (1955), profound explorations of the grounds for faith in God and ways of responding to God; *Man's Quest for God: Studies in Prayer and Symbolism* (1954), a collection of essays containing what many people regard as the most penetrating analysis of prayer written in twentieth-century America; *The Prophets* (1962), a monumental study that greatly expands the work on the prophets that he had done for his doctoral dissertation; *Who Is Man?* (1965), a cogent defense of the transcendent dignity of being human; *The Insecurity of Freedom: Essays on Human Existence* (1966), a collection of twenty essays dealing with issues such as race relations, medical care, the plight of the elderly, interfaith relations, and religious education; *Israel: An Echo of Eternity* (1968), an elegant explanation of the significance that Israel holds for Jews everywhere; and *A Passion for Truth* (1973), a remarkable comparative study of the Baal Shem Tov, the Kotzker Rebbe, and Danish philosopher Søren Kierkegaard.

Along with these widely read books he wrote in English, Heschel also wrote major works in Yiddish and Hebrew: a two-volume Yiddish work on the Kotzker Rebbe, never translated into English but whose title translates as *Kotzk: The Struggle for Integrity* (1973) and a three-volume Hebrew work (volume 1, 1962; volume 2, 1965; volume 3, 1990) exploring major issues of revelation according to different strands of rabbinic theology, translated into English by Gordon Tucker with Leonard Levin and recently published in one massive volume as *Heavenly Torah As Refracted through the Generations* (2005).

Heschel believed that "music is the soul of language" and that "a sentence without a tone, without a musical quality is like a body without a soul."[31] He made sure that the language he employed and the literary corpus he produced were full of soul. "His works are like enchanted forests," writes Fritz Rothschild. "If only we take the effort to enter them, we shall find them both enchanted and enchanting."[32] As such, Heschel's writings evoke the religious sensitivity, indeed the sense of God's presence, to which they bear witness.

These writings of Heschel's are genuinely religious because they reflect his authentic religious life: a harmony of prayer, study, and action. His action consisted primarily in the unsung ethical and religious deeds of a pious Jew, but he also took a public stand on a number of social issues. This began early in his life and was particularly evident in an anti-Nazi lecture he delivered in Germany in March 1938.[33]

Nevertheless, it was only in the last decade of his life that Heschel emerged as a recognized ethical leader of national and international prominence. This began in 1963 when he delivered the keynote address at the National Conference on Religion and Race, which led to widespread clergy participation in the great "march on Washington." He was passionate and persistent in his support of civil rights and in his condemnation of racism, which, as an "unmitigated evil," he considered "worse than idolatry."[34] He often appeared with Martin Luther King Jr., and he walked by his side in the great Selma-Montgomery march of 1965. Hailing Heschel as "one of the truly great men of our day and age" and "a truly great prophet," King explained his admiration by saying: "Rabbi Heschel is one of the persons who is relevant at all times, always standing with prophetic insights to guide us through these difficult days. He has been with us in many of our struggles."[35]

Heschel also protested the American involvement in the Vietnam War. Not only was he one of the earliest opponents of that war, but, according to Robert McAfee Brown, he was "*the* supreme Jewish voice and leader on Vietnam."[36] "To speak about God and remain silent on Vietnam is blasphemous," said Heschel.[37] And in the last years of his life he seemed to speak as much about Vietnam as he did about God. The renowned Protestant theologian John C. Bennett remembered how Heschel "never stopped pressing those questions" about how the American people could allow our country to perpetrate what he considered a terribly unjust war. "Two days before his death, the last time I was to hear his voice," recalled Bennett, "he spoke about the intensified bombing of North Vietnam, of the agony of Vietnam and of the shame of America and of the conflict in her soul."[38] Along with Bennett, Heschel had been one of the founders and a national cochairman of Clergy and Laity Concerned about Vietnam, a national interfaith organization that helped to bring the moral and religious implications of the Vietnam War to the attention of the American people. It was largely in connection with this organization that Heschel spent an enormous amount of time and energy in the service of peace. "His feeling for the God of pathos magnified his empathy with the Vietnamese victims," claims

Heschel's biographer, and "his opposition to the Vietnam War sapped his health."[39]

Heschel was also the first major Jewish figure to urge world Jewry to come to the aid of the Jews in the Soviet Union. "Early in the 1960s," writes Reuven Kimelman, "when Heschel was forging concern for Vietnam, he was simultaneously lighting the spark for one of the greatest protest movements of Jewish history—Soviet Jewry."[40] Due to increased antisemitic propaganda and actions in the Soviet Union, and to severe restrictions placed on their religious liberties by Soviet authorities, Jews there were suffering what Heschel called "spiritual genocide." At the 1963 convocation of the Rabbinical Assembly, Heschel cried out: "The six million are no more," referring to the Jews killed in the Holocaust. "Now three million face spiritual extinction. . . . Let the twentieth century not enter the annals of Jewish history as the century of physical and spiritual destruction!"[41] Recalling Heschel's address to the Assembly, Fritz Rothschild writes: "His passionate plea for massive public action received wide publicity in the press and led to the subsequent formation of the American Conference on Soviet Jewry."[42]

Heschel was also active and immensely influential in interfaith relations. Most noteworthy is the prominent role he assumed in the negotiations between Jewish organizations and the hierarchy of the Roman Catholic Church before and during the Second Vatican Council (1962–65). He was the most influential American Jewish delegate at the council, encouraging church leaders to condemn antisemitism, to eliminate anti-Judaism from church teachings, and to acknowledge the integrity and permanent preciousness of Judaism. Although the conciliar decree on interfaith relations, *Nostra Aetate*, did not fulfill Heschel's expectations, he acknowledged it as a landmark in the history of Catholic-Jewish relations.

Heschel also had far-reaching interfaith influence apart from formal interfaith dialogue. Through his writing, teaching, and public lecturing, he taught Jews and Christians to recognize the sanctity of each other's religion and he helped them to realize the mutual spiritual benefits of interfaith encounter. Living his last decade of life in the midst of an interfaith revolution he helped to create, Heschel had the opportunity to reach the Christian world in ways unknown to Jews of previous generations. And while he was one of many Jewish religious thinkers of the twentieth century to influence Christian thinking, he more than others fostered an enhanced appreciation of Judaism among Christians and, consequently, challenged them to rethink traditional Christian teachings about Judaism and about Christianity in relation to Judaism.

In the context of speaking about Heschel's influence on Christians, Robert McAfee Brown gave this personal testimony: "When I have been in his presence and have talked with him and have heard him pray, I have been moved to ask myself, 'What have I got to tell this man about God?' and thus far I have never found an answer. At this stage of Christian-Jewish dialogue I remain content to learn."[43]

To have inspired an outstanding Christian theologian to such an extent that he felt he had nothing to tell Heschel about God, and was therefore "content to learn" from him, was for Heschel to perform a major feat for Judaism in relation to Christianity. And what he did for Brown, Heschel did for many other Christians as well. He inspired them to appreciate the credibility and relevance of Jewish views of God and the abiding validity of Jewish covenantal life with God, which for nearly two thousand years Christians usually have refused to acknowledge.

Traditionally, Christian theologians have taught that the validity of Judaism came to an end with the emergence of Christianity as the one valid pathway to God. And one of the principal ways they have attempted to demonstrate the superiority of Christianity over Judaism has been to claim that Christian views of God are superior to Jewish views. By convincing many Christians that Jewish understandings of God are every bit as profound as what Christian theologians usually have claimed can be attained only by means of Christian faith, Heschel has helped them to appreciate the grandeur of the Jewish tradition. This, in turn, has compelled many Christians to rethink how they understand their Christian faith in relation to Judaism.

Unwavering in his commitment to one particular religion, Heschel nonetheless believed that "diversity of religions is the will of God,"[44] the theme explored in chapter 4 of this book. Through encounter with Heschel, many Christians have reached the same conclusion. Having had their faith in God enriched by a contemporary Jew devoted to his tradition, these Christians, however differently they may formulate their understanding of it, have come to believe that Judaism has abiding significance and that Christianity is valid not because it has superseded Judaism but because it, like Judaism, fosters covenantal life with God.

Of course, many Jews have inspired Christians to reconsider what they think about Judaism and about their own faith in relation to Judaism, but Heschel may well have inspired such reconsideration more than any other. This is mostly because he became—as he remains through his writings we are about to explore—a preeminent witness and guide to the reality and the relevance of God.

CHAPTER ONE

NATURE, HUMANITY, AND GOD

This chapter focuses on one of Abraham Heschel's principal tasks as a philosophical theologian: the exploration of how human experiences of nature and of our humanity convey the reality and presence of God and constitute grounds for faith in God.

Nature and Humanity Alluding to God

"How does one find a way to an awareness of God through beholding the world here and now?"[1] This is the opening question in a chapter titled "The Sublime" in one of Heschel's most important books. The answer he expounds there and elsewhere may be summarized as follows: by recognizing an aspect of reality that is often, perhaps even usually, ignored; by beholding the sublime dimension of this world, one may find a way to an awareness of God who is beyond, while present in, the world.

From Sublime Mystery to Divine Meaning

The grand premise of religion, according to Heschel, is that we human beings are able to surpass ourselves, and he suggests that it is in perceiving and appreciating the sublime that self-transcendence begins to occur. So Heschel begins his philosophy of religion where religion itself begins, with the sense of the sublime, which he also calls the awareness of grandeur.

Heschel claims there are three aspects of nature that command our attention: its power, its beauty, and its grandeur. Power we exploit; beauty we enjoy; grandeur, the sublime, fills us with wonder and awe.[2] Some authors have equated the sublime with the beautiful, while others have described the sublime in terms of the vast and magnificent in nature in contrast to the beautiful as having the qualities of delicacy, form, and color. For Heschel, however, the sublime is "the silent allusion of things to a meaning greater than themselves"[3] and may be sensed in the small and the great alike, in things of beauty, in human deeds, and in historic events.

Since the allusion to transcendent meaning is "silent," it is often not perceived or is easily ignored. The attention of any person or any society may focus or even fixate on a particular aspect of nature, which in turn may yield a given human accomplishment or culture. Sadly enough, many of us are preoccupied with nature's power or energy to such an extent that, while some appreciation of beauty remains, the sublimity of nature is hardly recognized. Consequently, nature's usefulness is deemed its foremost characteristic, and exploitation is our chief reply to nature's wealth. But it is unworthy of us to disregard the sublime, the sense of which is "the root of . . . creative activities in art, thought, and noble living."[4]

The fixation on the power aspect of nature and the consequent lack of appreciation for the sublime is bad for both nature and humanity—as the former is unsustainably exploited and the latter spiritually impoverished. Heschel therefore calls for a "radical reorientation" toward the sublime dimension of life in order to overcome the "instrumentalization" of the world and the consequent "disintegration" of genuine human living.[5] This requires what he calls "a sense for the inexpedient."[6] The way of expediency and exploitation, which is the result of fixating our attention on nature's power, prevents us from recognizing and appreciating the grandeur of nature. In order to sense the sublime we must "cultivate stillness in the soul."[7] The grandeur of nature unveils itself to a contemplative spirit rather than to a calculating mind, to a person who seeks to commune with nature, not simply control it.

To be sure, the exercise of power and the enjoyment of beauty are often legitimate pursuits and moral acts, and through these we may find degrees of meaning in life. But it is only when we perceive and respond to the sublime in life that we are on our way toward the ultimate meaning for which we long and in relation to which our lives will be fulfilled.

The fact that, for Heschel, the sublime is a "silent allusion" does not mean it is less real than it would be if it were blatant. It means, rather, that it is a spiritual quality of nature rather than a physical one. If the sublime is identified as either power or beauty, then it would be seen as a physical characteristic of nature that could be physically perceived. But as "an *allusiveness* to transcendent meaning," the sublime is "a spiritual suggestiveness of reality," a "spiritual radiance" that can be perceived only with spiritual sensitivity.[8]

This spiritual radiance of nature of which Heschel writes is attested to by another great philosopher, Alfred North Whitehead: "When you understand all about the sun and all about the atmosphere and all about the rotation of the earth, you may still miss the radiance of the sunset and the glory of the morning sky."[9] If it is possible to "miss the radiance," then it must be something more than physical luminosity. It is, rather, "the immense preciousness of being . . . which is not an object of analysis but a cause of wonder."[10] As such, this preciousness, this allusiveness to transcendent meaning, is a spiritual quality of nature that is spiritually perceived to be as real as nature's physical aspects through which it is known.

If nature has a spiritual radiance and thus alludes to transcendent meaning, how much more—at least for human beings—does humanity! This is because "the essence of being human is concern for transcendent meaning" and because of the uniquely human ways of expressing that concern—for example, in words that "are a repository of the spirit," in songs that carry our souls "to heights which utterable meanings can never reach," in music that is "an attempt to convey that which is within our reach but beyond our grasp," and in righteous deeds that "lead us to wells of emergent meaning, to experiences which are full of hidden brilliance of the holy."[11]

The holiness or sanctity of human life, the affinity of the divine and the human, and the disclosure of the divine in the human—these are the most consistently emphasized themes in and throughout Heschel's writings and they are summarized as follows: "Many things on earth are precious, some are holy, humanity is holy of holies. To meet a human being is an opportunity to sense the image of God, *the presence* of God."[12]

But how do we know that this perception of the sublime in nature and humanity is not illusory, like so many other perceptions are? Why believe there is more to nature and to human existence than their physical aspects that, so to speak, meet the eye? The "proof" of the perception is in the fruit it bears. The disavowal of the sublime spells human demise, while the affirmation of it yields enhancement of human life. Beholding the sublime dimension of existence "we become alive to our living in the great fellowship of all beings" and we are moved to ask: "Who are we to scan the esoteric stars, to witness the settings of the sun, to have the service of the spring for our survival? How shall we ever reciprocate for breathing and thinking, for sight and hearing, for love and achievement?"[13]

Yes, affirming the sublime, we seek not to exploit, and not simply to enjoy, but to reciprocate—and "*the dignity of human existence is in the power of reciprocity.*"[14] Is it not reasonable to believe that a perception that provokes dehumanization is the real illusion, while a perception that fosters human dignity reflects the truth? Is it not reasonable to believe that disavowing the sublime manifests "an undeveloped sense for the depth of things,"[15] while affirming it helps us to see things as they really are—as allusions to transcendent meaning, signals of the divine?

In any case, this perception of the sublime involves an awareness of mystery, for "what smites us with unquenchable amazement is not that which we grasp and are able to convey but that which lies within our reach but beyond our grasp."[16] Standing face-to-face with the grandeur of the world we are overcome with the realization that "the world is something *we apprehend but cannot comprehend*," that "the world is itself hiddenness; its essence is a mystery."[17] And the transcendent meaning to which the sublime alludes is "a meaning wrapped in mystery."[18]

There are people for whom life's exceptional events may contain an element of mystery but for whom life is for the most part explainable. Many human beings, and perhaps most of us at one time or another, act and talk as if being is something that can be taken for granted; that whatever is can be known and explained. Heschel counters this rationalist view: "To ex-plain means to make plain. Yet, the roots of existence are never plain, never flat; existence is anchored in *depth*."[19] As such, existence is a mystery: "What *is*, is more than what you see; what *is*, is 'far off and deep, exceedingly deep' [Eccl 7:24]. *Being is mysterious*."[20] The sublime dwells not only in the extraordinary and the remote but in the common-place and the intimate as well; and what is sublime is mysterious. "Every-where we encounter the mystery: in the rock and in the bee, in the cloud and in the sea."[21]

But does not science pierce the aura of enigma that Heschel assumes surrounds all things? Does it not at least diminish the mystery of many things once thought unfathomable? To be sure, science explains many previously unexplained aspects of things in this world, but it does not explain all there is to things, certainly not the mystery that abides in them and in which they abide. "The world as scrutinized and depicted by sci-ence is but a thin surface of the profoundly unknown."[22] And, more positively, "science extends rather than limits the scope of the ineffable, and our radical amazement is enhanced rather than reduced by the ad-vancement of knowledge," according to Heschel, who explains his view in this way: "Scientific research is an entry into the endless, not a blind alley; solving one problem, a greater one enters our sight. One answer breeds a multitude of new questions; explanations are merely indications of greater puzzles. Everything hints at something that transcends it. . . . What appears to be the center is but a point on the periphery of another center. The totality of things is actual infinity."[23]

This, of course, does not mean that the search for knowledge is futile. While everything abides in mystery, mystery is not everything. "The world is both open and concealed, a matter of fact and a mystery. We know and we do not know—this is our condition."[24]

Mystery engulfs everything, but our quest for knowledge is not drowned by mystery. On the contrary, the encounter with mystery is a prerequisite for intellectual endeavor and for the acquisition of knowledge. "All creative thinking comes out of *an encounter with the unknown*. We do not embark upon an investigation of what is definitely known. . . . It is in the awareness that the mystery we face is incomparably deeper than what we know that all creative thinking begins."[25] So the keener our sense of mystery is, the more acute our knowledge. And the more we attain true knowledge, the more we see mystery everywhere, even within our knowledge. Real knowledge, or what is better called wisdom, is not a triumph over mystery but a rapport with the mystery—and with the meaning for which it stands.

To have "an encounter with the unknown" is, paradoxically, to somehow know the unknown; it involves an awareness without comprehension. To know the mystery is not just to sense its existence; yet it is not a matter of comprehending its essence. To know the mystery is to have an insight into its meaningfulness without being able to penetrate its meaning. In acknowledging the mystery we realize that we are meant "not to measure meaning in terms of our own mind" and we begin "to sense a meaning infinitely greater than ourselves."[26]

"Everything holds the great secret. For it is the inescapable situation of all being to be involved in the infinite mystery. We may continue to disregard the mystery, but we can neither deny nor escape it."[27] We certainly cannot escape the mystery by withdrawing into the confines of the self. As human beings we not only have a sense of mystery, we ourselves are a great mystery unto ourselves. "What we are, we cannot say; what we become, we cannot grasp."[28]

"Many of us are conscious of the hiddenness of things, but few of us sense the mystery of our own presence. The self cannot be described in terms of the mind, for all our symbols are too poor to render it. The self is more than we dream of; it stands, as it were, with its back to the mind. Indeed, to the mind, even the mind itself is more enigmatic than a star."[29] In short, "the most intimate is the most mysterious."[30]

Belonging to the Divine

The awareness of the self's mysterious nature prompts the realization that "the self did not originate in itself" and, therefore, "that existence is not a property but a trust," that "*I am what is not mine.*"[31] Humbled by this realization, I am moved to ask: How did the self that I am originate? Who "owns" the existence with which I have been entrusted? To whom does the self that is not mine belong?

Did I originate from my parents? Were they the ultimate source of my self? No, parents are life's creative participants, not the primary source of life and its creativity. "In generating life, we are the tools, not the masters."[32] My parents gave me life, but it was life that they received.

Does the self, whose existence is a trust rather than a property of the self, belong to any human being, to any society of human beings, or to humanity as a whole? No, for if there is any principle of which we humans are intuitively certain, it is that no person belongs to—in the sense of being rightly possessed by—any other person, any society, or even the human race itself.

If my self, or any human self, did not originate in itself, it is reasonable to believe that humanity did not originate in itself. Humanity, according to Heschel, "is not conceived as a species, as an abstract concept, stripped from its concrete reality, but as an abundance of specific individuals."[33] It is therefore just as legitimate to inquire to whom humanity belongs as it is to ask to whom the self belongs. If *I am what is not mine*, then *humanity is not its own*.

While we humans are accountable to each other, humanity and every human being or group of human beings—even though free to acknowledge it or not, to act in accord with it or not—are ultimately accountable to the creative reality that transcends humanity, that entrusts it with existence, and that challenges and empowers human beings to be trustworthy in and with existence. The transcendent source of human existence is present to human beings, individually and collectively, as the challenge "to live in a way which is compatible with the grandeur and mystery of living"[34] and as the empowering spirit that animates life and enables human beings to live up to that challenge.

But what is this challenging and empowering source of human existence? Is it nature, or any other power in the world? Of this are we not certain, that although we are a part of nature we somehow also transcend nature? How could nature be our ultimate origin if we as human beings in some respects transcend it? And since "nature is deaf to our cries and indifferent to our values,"[35] how could it be said that ultimately we belong to nature?

Since humanity did not originate in itself and is therefore *not its own*, and since it is "a personal reality,"[36] it must have originated in and ultimately belong to a personal reality that transcends it. And since the world is not a personal reality, humanity must have its origin in a reality that transcends the world. We know the world is not the ultimate reality, that it is not divine, precisely because it is not a personal reality and because it cannot account for its own existence. Might it not be dependent on the same transcendent reality on which humanity must ultimately depend for its existence?

If it is reasonable to assume that humanity, though originating within the world, has its ultimate origin in a source beyond the world, is it not also reasonable to assume that the world has the same transcendent source? This, indeed, is what Heschel assumes—that humanity and the world "have a mystery in common: the mystery of being dependent upon meaning," upon the "meaning of all meanings,"[37] which is one of Heschel's ways of referring to God.

To realize our dependence upon God as "the meaning of all meanings" is to know that we are not ultimately dependent on any partial meaning—or any finite vehicle of meaning, including the whole community of finite beings. We are, instead, ultimately dependent on "*being in and beyond all beings.*"[38] This is what Heschel means when he says: "Our life is not our own property but a possession of God. And it is this divine ownership that makes life a sacred thing."[39]

Rightly, we reject the idea that any person may be possessed or owned by another person, by any society, or even by the whole human race. Should we not also reject the idea that our life is a possession of God? Of course, some of us do reject this idea. But might that rejection be due to thinking of God along the lines of finite being? It would be life-stifling to be possessed by any finite being or community of beings, but is it not liberating to think that we belong to the Infinite? (Perhaps Heschel should have spoken only of "belonging to God" rather than also speaking of "divine ownership" or of our life as "a possession of God," because saying that we belong to someone or to a community does not necessarily imply our feeling owned or possessed by them; it may, on the contrary, imply our feeling of love or communal identity. But, as suggested below, given Heschel's understanding of God, by "divine ownership" he certainly does not mean to imply anything similar to human ownership, and by calling our life "a possession of God" he does not intend to suggest this is anything like feeling as though we are in the possession of another human being or a human community.)

If God is understood as "being in and beyond all beings," as "the meaning of all meanings," then to acknowledge "divine ownership" of our being is to recognize that no partial meaning, no finite being or community of finite beings, is our ultimate horizon of being and meaning. It is, in other words, to open ourselves "to the mystery and transcendence of living."[40]

Taken out of context, Heschel's idea of "divine ownership," of our life as "a possession of God," might be misunderstood as suggesting that God limits our freedom. But since Heschel perceives God as the very source of human freedom, his speaking of "divine ownership" of life is one of his ways—perhaps a way too prone to being misunderstood—of suggesting that nothing in the world and not even the world itself can be the limit of our longing, that our souls are free to soar beyond the world's horizon. "All thoughts and feelings about the tangible and knowable world do not exhaust the endless stirring within us. There is a surplus of restlessness over our palpable craving. . . . What is the essence of our feeling for God? May it not be defined as a yearning that knows no satisfaction, as a yearning to meet that which we do not even know how to long for?"[41]

Heschel knew this yearning throughout his life. Here he expresses it in one of his early poems: "First you created longing, / then later earth and heaven. / And a home for us? No, not yet! / Every nearness / Is too far for us. / Distance—breakdown of the universe, / Thrust away distance! / I am a trace of You in the world, / and everything is like a door. / Let us all trace that trace of You, and through all things go to You."[42]

In a book much later in life, immediately after referring to God as "*being in and beyond all beings*," Heschel writes as if in mystical rapture: "A tremor seizes our limbs; our nerves are struck, quiver like strings; our whole being bursts into shudders. But then a cry, wrested from our very core, fills the world around us. . . . It is one word: GOD. . . . The word that means more than universe, more than eternity, holy, holy, holy; we cannot comprehend it."[43] This Reality, and not anything less, is the reality to whom we ultimately belong and in relation to whom we realize our true freedom as human beings. Those who are "in bondage to environment, to social ties, to inner disposition, may yet enjoy freedom before God."[44] To choose "a life of utmost striving for the utmost stake, the vital, matchless stake of God"[45] is an act of faith that lifts us beyond any limiting horizon of being and meaning.

Experiencing the Presence of God

When, perceiving the sublime mystery of existence, we sense that nature and humanity dwell within a horizon of being and meaning that exceeds human creativity and comprehension, there is no escaping the question of God. As an academic issue, the question of God can be avoided. As an existential issue, the question of God insinuates itself into our souls; we sense it as "a question addressed to us"[46] rather than one we raise on our own accord. And with this sense of divine address may come a sense, an experience, of divine presence.

Ultimate Meaning as Transcendent Presence

Throughout his writings, Heschel repeatedly suggests that we human beings constitutionally crave a sense of meaning; not just a sense that facets of existence have particular meanings but that existence as such has ultimate meaning. And he argues that this ultimate meaning, to be truly ultimate, can be nothing less than an ultimate presence: "Ultimate meaning as an idea [rather than a presence] is no answer to our anxiety. Humanity is more than an intellectual structure; it is a personal reality. The cry for meaning is a cry for ultimate relationship, for ultimate belonging."[47] Only a personal reality may serve as the ultimate meaning for another personal reality, and therefore the ultimate question is not "*What* is the meaning of human being?" but rather "*Who* is our ultimate meaning, or *Who* is our God?"

The answer obviously cannot be nature because, unlike humanity, nature is not a personal reality. So with full appreciation for the grandeur of nature, Heschel affirms the reality of God as distinct from, though intimately present to, the world of nature. Neither can humanity, nor any human being or group of human beings, be the ultimate meaning for any of us, because being human involves responding to meaning not simply made by human beings. By responding to this transcendent meaning we human beings surpass ourselves; by failing to respond we sink below the level of the genuinely human.

Spellbound by the splendor of existence, by the marvel of our own existence, humbled by the fact that we often fail to realize the meaning within the marvel, we human beings must confess that we are not sovereign in the realm of being, that we have not authored the realm of meaning. Only a reality beyond the world of nature and humanity can be the ultimate source of all being and meaning. And only an ultimate presence—a transcendent personal reality—can be ultimately meaningful to us as personal beings oriented toward this ultimate meaning.

But how do we know ultimate meaning as ultimate presence? Finding ourselves involved in the inescapable context of meaning, we come to realize that meaning is something we discover rather than something we simply crave or invent, that it is "meaning that drives us to think about meaning."[48] Realizing this, we sense that our anxiety about meaning is "a response to a challenge."[49] We also sense that this challenge must issue from a source that transcends humanity because it seems to us that all human beings, individually and collectively, those who recognize it and those who do not, live under the challenge.

We come to know transcendent meaning as a divine presence, as "a transcendence called the living God," because "that transcendence is not a passive thing; it is a challenging transcendence."[50] And this challenging transcendence signifies "transcendent concern," because there would be no challenge to us without a concern for us.[51] This challenging and concerned transcendence is what Heschel means by God. As such, God is the ultimate meaning in whose presence we find meaning by responding to the divine challenge to share in divine concern for all beings.

But it is not only as a challenge that the divine concern is known but also as the empowering source of our responsiveness to that challenge. Our concern for other human beings, for example, is at times experienced as a concern with which we are endowed, a blessing of transcendent origin. Those who know the wonder and mystery of caring for others should be able to understand what Heschel means when he says that "our life is felt to be an overflowing of something greater than ourselves, the excess of a spirit not our own."[52]

Driven to the Question of God

Awestruck by the realization that we are recipients of life, its participants and witnesses rather than its authors, we know ourselves to be driven to the question of God. It is not only our sense of finitude in the face of grandeur that forces us to confront this question but also "the realization of our own great spiritual power, the power to heal what is broken in the world."[53] Since this spiritual power is experienced as something instilled within us rather than originated by us, we realize that God's concern, more than ours, accounts for the unavoidable question of God.

We are driven to the question of God "because the world is replete with what is more than the world as we understand it," because we are "introduced to a reality which is not only *other* than ourselves . . . but which is *higher* than the universe," because we "learn to sense that all existence is embraced by a spiritual presence."[54] The situation that accounts for the existential question of God is one in which we are stunned by the mysterious grandeur of the world, struck by the miraculous wonder of our own existence and that of others, and confronted by a presence so challenging and empowering that we feel compelled to identify it as divine.

We know that the question *about* God is ultimately a question *from* God because it is an "invincible question," one that pursues us even when we may not wish to pursue it. "We cannot question the supreme invincible question that extends in front of us, opening itself to us like time, unremittingly, and pleading with us like a voice that had been melted into stillness."[55]

Who among us would dare to raise such a question on our own, a question that tears our world asunder, depriving us of all complacency and self-satisfaction? And who among us has the spiritual strength to answer that question? Is not such an invincible question evidence for the reality of a transcendent challenge? Is not our responding to it evidence for the reality of an empowering transcendent concern? And could such transcendent challenge and concern be anything but divine?

Not in Heschel's view. For him, the existential question of God, experienced as an invincible question, is evidence enough of the presence and reality of God. "When all our mind is aglow with the eternal question like a face in gazing on a mighty blaze, we are not moved to ask: Where is God?" No, in that context we ask "Where are we?" and are moved to confess that "God is more plausible than our own selves."[56]

This, indeed, is the epitome of Heschel's religious insight: the presence of God is more credible than our own presence, the reality of God more plausible than our own existence. And since God's presence is sensed as transcendent concern and challenge, this means that God's concern for us is more plausible than our concern for God, that God's challenge to us precedes and provokes whatever questions we have about God.

Manifold Experiences of One God

But might not the manifold experiences of transcendent concern and challenge testify to a multiplicity of concerned and challenging deities rather than to one and the same God? From Heschel's perspective, the answer is *no* for the following reason. Since the manifold experiences of the transcendent concern and transcendent challenge about which he writes are all experiences of a unifying concern, of a challenge "to keep aflame our awareness of living in the great fellowship of all beings,"[57] for this reason the manifold experiences must be testifying to the presence of one creative source of unity, one unifying force or power, one God. Although experienced in myriad ways, the transcendent concern and challenge that drives us toward oneness must be supremely one. "Political and moral unity as a goal presupposes unity as a source."[58]

This is how we know whether or not our religious experiences are genuine experiences of the divine: "Oneness is the norm, the standard and the goal."[59] If a religious experience inspires us to work for unity where there is discord, then we can trust that it is, in some sense, an experience of the divine source of all unity. If, on the other hand, an experience inclines us toward divisiveness, we can know that it is a deviation from the divine. "Evil is *divergence*, confusion, that which alienates . . . while good is *convergence*, togetherness, *union*," writes Heschel, and "unity of God is power for the unity of God with all things."[60]

The experiences of transcendent concern and challenge that Heschel depicts empower us to work for unity. As such, they all point to the presence of one God: "There is no insight more disclosing: *God is One, and humanity is one.*"[61] This is why, for example, racial prejudice is "a treacherous denial of the existence of God."[62] And because the one God is concerned not only with all human beings but with all creatures, authentic experiences of God's presence are those that foster a sense for "the sacred relevance of all being" and for *"the togetherness of all beings in holy otherness."*[63]

"The world lies in strife," says Heschel, but "the vision of the One, upon which we stake our effort and our ultimate hope," is the vision of the God who is "subdued yet present everywhere, giving us the power to aid in bringing about ultimate unification."[64]

The Ethical Core of the Experience of God

From the above, it is clear that, for Heschel, genuine religious experience necessarily involves moral awareness—and this is something worth stressing for at least two reasons: first, because many religious believers, while perhaps seeing morality as a component of religion, are at pains to distinguish religious experience from ethical awareness; and, second, because many ethicists who disavow religion are equally insistent that moral awareness, often existing apart from religious commitment, is not to be confused with religious consciousness.

But, in Heschel's view, genuine moral sensitivity, because it involves a sense for "the sacred relevance of all being," is intrinsically religious; and, conversely, authentic religious experience is intrinsically moral. Heschel makes this explicit by claiming that the sense of divine presence "does not find its fulfillment in esthetic contemplation; it is astir with a demand to live in a way that is worthy of that presence."[65]

Understandably, those who do not believe in God tend not to speak of their appreciation for the sacredness of life as a religious appreciation rooted in religious experience. (In fact, many agnostics and atheists may hesitate to speak of their moral sensitivity as an appreciation for the *sacredness* of life.) But it is not only agnostics and atheists who think of moral awareness as something separate from religious experience. While having a sense of the sacredness of being, many believers in God speak of having no *experience* of God. But from Heschel's perspective, a sense of the sacred, and a sense of having to live in a way that is consonant with this sense of the sacred, may be described as an experience of God's presence.

People who sense the sacred and their obligation to live in accord with the sacred but nonetheless think they do not experience God's presence may be expecting that presence to be too much like a human presence. But because God's being "transcends mysteriously all conceivable being,"[66] God's presence transcends all other types of presence. It is, so to speak, a disguised presence. As Heschel puts it: "In every soul there lives incognito a coercion to love."[67] And this, precisely, is the test of authentic religious experience: whether or not it inspires us to love. "Beyond all mystery is the mercy of God. It is a love, a mercy that transcends the world, its value and merit. To live by such a love, to reflect it . . . is the test of religious existence."[68]

"God reaches us as a claim,"[69] says Heschel, a claim upon our conscience. But because the presence of God is incognito, people who experience the claim may not identify it as divine. And, of course, some of the specific demands of conscience, rather than being from God, have the marks of being self-imposed or of representing internalized social demands.

Heschel realizes that self or society may spawn specific demands of conscience, but he suggests that this does not mean we are accountable solely to self or society. "Our sense of what is right and wrong may at times be uncertain. What is indubitably certain is our sense of obligation to answer for our conduct."[70] And what we sense is not only that we must answer to self and society for our conduct but that both we and society must answer to what transcends us. Thus, for Heschel, "the transcendent God" is the ultimate reality "to Whom our conscience is open."[71]

There can be no doubting the fact that, for Heschel, God is beyond our conscience: "We are guilty of committing the fallacy of misplacement. We define . . . conscience and call it God."[72] Yet Heschel also believes that our conscience may be open to God. It may be misguided and misguiding, but it may also be a locus of experiencing God: "There is a question that follows me wherever I turn. What is expected of me? What is demanded of me? What we encounter is not only flowers and stars, mountains and walls. Over and above all things is a sublime expectation."[73]

And what is the expectation? It is that we, in many and various ways, day in and day out, strive to live by imperatives like overcoming prejudice, coming to the aid of those who are suffering, and fostering unity and peace between and among people—and thereby to live "a life compatible with God's presence."[74]

But, as indicated earlier, God's presence reaches us not only as a transcendent expectation or challenge; it may also be sensed as transcendent care and concern. While for most of us this may be rare and fleeting, for some people God's "care and concern are a constant experience."[75] They feel, as Heschel says, "embraced by God's mercy as by a vast encircling space," and the presence of God is experienced "as peace, power and endless tranquility, as an inexhaustible source of help, as boundless compassion."[76]

But because "the guiding hand is hidden," most of us may not think that, ultimately, we are "guided by the mysterious hand of God."[77] God guides us by empowering others to show us the way, by inspiring us to see the way. The "hand of God" is a metaphor for divine guidance, and so we should not expect to feel that "hand" like we feel human hands— nor feel it apart from human hands.

Likewise, the "voice of God" is not an audible voice, and so we should not think we hear it apart from human voices that might mediate divine inspiration. We should need "no miraculous communication to make [us] aware of God's presence."[78] Divine guidance normally comes to us— indeed, in ways that are normal—through other human beings who are inspired by God to give guidance.

Thus, divine concern usually is not experienced apart from human concern, but it is the way that human concern is experienced—as concern with which we are empowered—that reveals the presence of the divine within it. When, with Heschel, we realize that we have within us "more compassion than [our] nerves can bear,"[79] we know that human compassion is a divine gift and a reflection of divine presence. "God is within the world, present and concealed," writes Heschel, yet "the human is the disclosure of the divine"—especially because human beings "may act in the likeness of God."[80]

For Heschel, there is a sense in which God is never absent from the world: "God's relation to the world is an actuality, . . . obtaining even if at this moment it is not perceived or acknowledged by anybody; those who reject or betray it do not diminish its validity. . . . All existence stands before God—here and everywhere, now and at all times."[81] Yet in another sense, he says, "it is as easy to expel God as it is to shed blood."[82] God's ubiquitous and abiding presence has to do with "God's infinite concern [that] is present in the world."[83] God's absence from human life has to do with the absence of human concern for God and God's will. It is incumbent upon us to be "present to the presence of God," and to be truly present is to live "a life compatible with God's presence."[84]

Affirming the Reality of God

So it is the presence of God, and not just the sublime mystery of the world, that drives us to the question of God's reality and to belief in God. Thus we can understand Heschel's claim that "God is a presupposition as well as a conclusion."[85] We accept the reality of God as the conclusion or the answer to the question of God only if God is the presupposition or basis of the question, only if God confronts us with the question. "Unless God asks the question, all our inquiries are in vain."[86] But inquire we do, as also we conclude, and so Heschel makes a distinction between *experiencing* the presence of God and *affirming* the reality of God. For him, the affirmation of the existence of God is a consequence of having been stirred by the presence of God.

The Reality and Divinity of the Transcendent Presence

Heschel accepts Immanuel's Kant's doctrine that existence cannot be reached through thought alone, that there is no warrant for postulating the existence of a reality on the basis of an idea of that reality within the mind. And he, like Kant, applies this doctrine to the question of God's existence: "The most basic objection to the belief in the existence of God is the argument that such a belief passes from the mind's data to something that surpasses the scope of the mind. What gives us the assurance that an idea which we may find ourselves obliged to think may hold true of a reality that lies beyond the reach of the mind? Such an objection is valid when applied to the speculative approach."[87]

Here Heschel (along with Kant) may be challenged. It may be argued that the very fact that Heschel speaks of "an idea which we may find ourselves *obliged* to think" indicates, contrary to what he suggests, that the idea does "hold true of a reality that lies beyond the reach of the mind." To be sure, we are *not obliged* to have an idea of a finite object that we or other reliable sources have not encountered, and therefore the thought of someone or something finite, like Santa Claus or a unicorn, is no guarantee of its existence. But if we are aware of existence at all, then we *are obliged*, upon reflecting on the grounds for the possibility of finite or contingent existence, to have an idea of a necessary existence without which finite beings would not be. And if such an idea is one we are obliged to think, then is it not valid to deduce from this idea "a reality that lies beyond the reach of the mind," a Reality unlike any other reality?

But even if, contrary to what Heschel suggests, this speculative deduction concerning the reality of God is valid, it does not foster the kind of affirmation about God's reality that Heschel himself champions. In his words: "The certainty of the realness of God does not come about as a corollary of logical premises, as a leap from the realm of logic to the realm of ontology, from an assumption to a fact. . . . In asserting: God is, we merely bring down overpowering reality to the level of thought. Our thought is but an after-belief."[88]

If "our thought is but an after-belief," our belief is but an after-experience. It is the actual experience of the presence of God that gives rise to our belief in the reality of God and our attempt, however fallibly, to articulate that belief. The experience of God's presence is the experience of a *real* presence. And so the affirmation of God's reality is a consequence of experiencing that reality. We affirm the existence of God because we experience a presence so overpowering that its reality cannot be denied and so empowering that its divinity must be confessed.

Note, we not only affirm the *reality* of transcendent presence; we also confess its *divinity*. And what makes this reality divine is, primarily, that it is the transcendent concern for being without which being would cease, without which we would be devoid of the concern that makes life livable. According to Heschel, "the essence of life is intense care and concern,"[89] and he describes two different kinds of concern that constitute or foster life: *reflexive concern*, which is directed toward the self, and *transitive concern*, which is directed to others.[90] While human beings exhibit both types of concern, Heschel claims that it is only transitive concern than can be ascribed to God.[91]

Heschel repeatedly points out that we human beings cannot comprehend the essence of God, but he nonetheless indicates that we need to speak not only about God's existence but also about God's essence: "Existence . . . cannot be imagined *per se*, unqualified, in utter nakedness; it is always some particular, specific existent, or mode of existence, a being dressed in attributes, that we grasp."[92] Thus, it is not the unqualified existence of God that Heschel asserts but, rather, the reality of God whose various attributes such as justice, mercy, and love are summed up in the term "transitive concern."

Heschel's claim that we can know the attributes of God seems to contradict his claim that God's essence is indescribable. But these two claims can be reconciled by way of a distinction he makes between two kinds of words: "*descriptive* words which stand in a fixed relation to conventional and definite meanings . . . and *indicative* words which stand in a fluid relation to ineffable meanings and, instead of describing, merely intimate something which we intuit but cannot fully comprehend."[93] The term "transitive concern," when applied to God, like the word "God" itself, is an indicative term, one that gives us an intimation of a meaning we "cannot fully comprehend."

Heschel is painfully aware of the inadequacy of all terms when applied to God, yet he is also cognizant of our need to use words to indicate what we understand by the reality of God. "God's existence—what may it mean?"[94] asks Heschel. And here is one of his answers: "God in the universe is a spirit of concern for life. What is a thing to us is a concern to God; what is a part of the physical world of being is also a part of a divine world of meaning. *To be* is *to stand for*, to stand for a divine concern."[95]

Divine Concern as a Credible Idea

Throughout his writings Heschel puts more emphasis on the experience of divine concern than on the concept of it, but he nonetheless also speaks of divine concern as a credible philosophical idea. Of course, it is primarily because the experience is so compelling that the idea is so commanding. But Heschel also regards the idea of divine concern to be philosophically tenable even apart from the profound experience of it that he portrays. This is because, for him, the idea of creation, which implies a transcendent concern for the world, is more persuasive that the idea that the world is self-sufficient.

While the idea of creation is reasonable even apart from the overwhelming experience of God's challenging concern as depicted by Heschel, it is nonetheless rooted in what he describes as our experience of radical amazement "*at the unexpectedness of being as such*, at the fact that there is being at all."[96] This is the opposite of merely accepting being at face value, which, in effect, is a way of regarding it as final or ultimate.

"The acceptance of the ultimacy of being," says Heschel, "mistakes a problem for a solution. The supreme and ultimate issue is not *being* but the *mystery* of being. Why is there being at all instead of nothing? We can never think of any being without conceiving the possibility of it not being. We are exposed to the presence as well as the absence of being."[97] As such, "realizing the contingency of being," we must "never identify being with ultimate reality."[98]

Aware of the unexpectedness or mystery of being, we realize that the "solution" is not to be found in the theory of the self-sufficiency of the world's being but in the doctrine of creation. "Being points to the question of how being is possible. The act of bringing being into being, creation, stands higher in the ladder of problems than being. Creation is not a transparent concept. But is the concept of being as being distinguished by lucidity? Creation is a mystery; being as being an abstraction."[99]

When Heschel speaks of the creation of being he is, of course, referring not to divine being but to the world of being, of which we are a part. "The mind dares to go behind being in asking about the source of being. It is true that the concept of that source implies being, yet it is also true that a Being that calls a reality into being is endowed with the kind of being that transcends mysteriously all conceivable being."[100] So while we are compelled to ask about the source of conceivable being, of the world of beings, it does not make sense to ask about the source of the Being that transcends all conceivable being, the Being that calls the world of beings into being.

The creation of the world of being is indeed a mystery, but the doctrine of creation is a more reasonable answer to the question of why there is being at all, why there is a world, than is the theory of the self-sufficiency of the world. In Heschel's words: "Is not the self-sufficiency of nature a greater puzzle, transcending all explanations, than the idea of nature's being dependent on what surpasses nature? The idea of dependence is an explanation, whereas self-sufficiency is an unprecedented, nonanalogous concept in terms of what we know about life within nature. Is not self-sufficiency itself insufficient to explain self-sufficiency?"[101]

Being in the world is not just a matter of *being as such*, explained in terms of self-sufficiency, but of *being as creation*, explained in terms of dependency. But the latter "explanation" is not to be mistaken for a scientific explanation. In truth, to be consistent, Heschel would have to admit it is not really an explanation but rather an allusion to transcendent meaning, a meaning that surpasses all conceivable meanings, a meaning that can be only be sensed but never comprehended. "The moment we utter the name of God we leave the level of scientific thinking and enter the realm of the ineffable. Such a step is one which we cannot take scientifically, since it transcends the boundaries of all that is given."[102]

If thinking about God is not a matter of scientific thinking, then concern about God's creation is not a scientific problem. In fact, it is not even a purely speculative or philosophical problem; it is, rather, a religious problem. Thus, Heschel rejects the classical "argument from design" that infers the existence of a creator from design in and of the universe as an adequate way of responding to the religious question of creation. The religious question is not about *how* the world came into being (for example, by way of an "intelligent design") but about *why* it is and *what* or *who* is its source of being and meaning. "The mystery of creation rather than the concept of design; a God that stands above the mystery rather than a designer or a master mind; a God in relation to Whom the world here and now may gain meaning—these are answers that are adequate to the religious problem."[103]

As a question of ultimate concern, the religious question reflects existential concern for the meaning of being. And Heschel believes that the doctrine of creation answers this question not by offering a comprehensible scientific or philosophical solution but by suggesting that being in the world points beyond itself to the mystery of transcendent or divine concern by which it came into being and by which it is sustained. It is this divine concern that is the fundamental category of Heschel's philosophical theology, summarized as follows: "Being is either open to, or dependent on, what is more than being, namely, care for being, or it is a cul-de-sac, to be explained in terms of self-sufficiency. . . . There is a care that hovers over being. Being is surpassed by concern for being. Being would cease to be were it not for God's care for being."[104]

The fact that Heschel believes that God creates and cares for the world of being does not mean that he thinks God controls all that goes on in the world.[105] In his view, the world's transcendent source is not the only world-shaping reality. The world that God creates is a world teeming with creatures that, in their various forms of freedom, affect the course of events in this world and thereby help to shape the world itself. Divine concern, not divine control, is the fundamental category of his philosophical theology.

But however much Heschel champions the *idea* of divine concern as implied in the concept of creation, it is, as we have seen, the *experience* of divine concern that he emphasizes even more. Nevertheless, this idea, when shown to be philosophically tenable, may lend support to the belief that the experience of divine concern is genuine and not illusory. But philosophical support is no substitute for the belief that is supported, nor for the experience that gives rise to the belief. It is, therefore, divine concern as an experience, more than the idea of it, that is a source of faith in God.

CHAPTER TWO

GOD'S REVELATION
TO THE JEWISH PEOPLE

Chapter 1 shows that, even apart from the revelation of God attested to in the Bible, Heschel considers it reasonable to believe in the reality and concern of one transcendent God. Nevertheless, Heschel's religious perspective, including the subject matter of our first chapter, is specifically Jewish and thus inspired by biblical testimonies of God's revelation, especially the revelation of God to and through the prophets of ancient Israel. To Heschel's understanding of this historic revelation we now turn.

The Meaning and Mystery of Revelation

The Jewish tradition emerged in response to revelatory events, and Jews keep their tradition alive by recounting and celebrating these events, by demonstrating their significance for the present and the future, and by relating them to current experiences of God's presence. Accordingly, much of Heschel's writing is devoted to the eventful nature of revelation and to the credibility of believing in revelation, mysterious as it is.

Revelation as an Event

"The God of the prophets was the God of events: the Redeemer from slavery, the Revealer of the Torah," writes Heschel, and "revelation is an event that does not happen all the time but at a particular time, at a unique moment of time."[1] As an event, the revelation of God, according to Heschel, is different than a process.

Heschel describes this distinction between a process and an event in the following way: "A process happens regularly, following a relatively permanent pattern; an event is extraordinary, irregular. A process may be continuous, steady, uniform; events happen suddenly, intermittently, occasionally. Processes are typical; events are unique. A process follows a law, events create a precedent."[2] Having made this distinction, Heschel goes on to point out that processes occur in the realm of nature, while events are what constitute history. God is present in and through the processes of nature, but God's special revelation to and through the prophets occurred in and through historical events. And since a process may be continuous while "events happen suddenly, intermittently, occasionally," Heschel rejects the idea of a "continuous revelation."[3]

This does not mean that Heschel rejects the idea of revelation continuing beyond the biblical period. To the contrary, he asserts: "The word of God never comes to an end. No word is God's last word."[4] Heschel acknowledges that divine revelation is not always and everywhere available to us, but he also insists that we must not assume it has come to an end. Although not continuously revealing, God does, from time to time, continue to communicate with us.

Another clarification is in order. As apt as is the distinction between a natural process and a historical event, it is also true that there are historical events that, process-like, unfold over time. But unlike natural processes, these historical process-like events involve acts of freedom, decision, and responsibility. If God is revealed in and through historical events, and if some events are what might be considered events-in-process, then perhaps it would not be inappropriate to speak of a process of revelation. Nevertheless, with Heschel, it seems important to recognize that since revelation does not occur automatically, even if it might at times be an event-in-process, it is a very different sort of process than any natural process.

According to Heschel, in the biblical tradition revelation is "not thought of as proceeding out of God like rays out of the sun" but as a divine "decision to disclose what otherwise would remain concealed."[5] This, it seems, is what Heschel is really driving at when he claims that revelation is an event as opposed to a process. Again, it is will and decision that make it an event, not that it happens "suddenly, intermittently, occasionally."

But even if revelation may be considered an event-in-process, does this mean that revelation may also be considered continuous? Perhaps in principle it could be, but in fact it appears not to be the case. There seem to be revelatory process-like events that occur from time to time rather than one uninterrupted revelatory event-in-process. Although God is always present, God's presence is not always evident. Although God is always concerned with humanity, God's will is not always communicated to human beings. Why? Perhaps it is because human beings are not always open to the presence and the will of God, and there can be no revelation unless human beings are attentive to God.

But is this the only reason that revelation is not continuous? There are many times when human beings are quite attentive, straining for a sign of God's presence, longing for a glimpse of the divine will, and yet receive no revelation from God. God may be ever present, but it seems that God is at times awfully silent. "My tears have been my food day and night, while people say to me continually, 'Where is your God?'" (Ps 42:3).

Heschel is aware of God's silence. In the happenings of history, he says, "we hear the voice as well as the silence of God."[6] Perhaps he puts it most poignantly in one of his early poems: "God, answer us—we long for You! / Overcome Your silence, Lord of all words! / . . . Deeper than my faith is the world's despair, / so that I'd give away all Your gifts to me and all my talents, / for simply a light bright word given from You."[7] To be sure, faith, which Heschel's poem unmistakably conveys, knows not God's continuous revelation.

But though there is not a continuous divine revelation, there indeed may be a continuous human faith in the divine. For faith is not simply responsiveness to God at times of divine revelation; it is also faithfulness to God during times of divine silence.[8] But faith *despite* the silence of God can be attained only *because* of a former divine revelation. Faith, as faithfulness, must rely on the remembrance of what has been disclosed.

"The Spirit of God speaks intermittently through the events of history, and our life is a continual wrestling with the Spirit," writes Heschel. "Whenever our historical memory becomes dim, the forsaken Spirit shakes us, and we know once more that we are servants by the grace of God."[9] Faith is the art of responding to God in moments of divine revelation and, as God's servants, of bearing witness to God in moments of divine silence. "You are meant to help here, Oh God!" cries Heschel in another of his poems. "But you are silent, while needs shriek. / So help me to help! I'll fulfill Your duty, / pay Your debts."[10]

In fact, is this not one of the principal ways that God speaks or acts, by empowering human beings to fulfill divine duties? If, as Heschel claims, "God's silence does not go on forever,"[11] is it not largely because

God inspires human beings to speak and to act prophetically on behalf of God?

The Credibility of Revelation

God's presence in the world is often concealed, but "there are moments in which it is revealed, particularly to the prophets"[12] of ancient Israel. Consistent with what we saw in chapter 1, the fact that Heschel says God's presence is revealed *particularly* to the prophets implies that he believes it is revealed *not only* to the prophets, though to them especially. The revelatory events experienced by the prophets may have been unique and unprecedented, but these events were not totally different from revelatory experiences that others have known.

"There is a grain of the prophet in the recesses of every human existence," says Heschel, "a degree of the prophetic senses"[13] that enabled the people of Israel to trust Moses and the prophets and enables us to accept the biblical message. To share the prophetic sense is to share in not only the prophetic task but also, to some degree, the prophetic experience of the revelatory presence of God. In fact, it is the prophetic experience that gives impetus to the prophetic task.

Nevertheless, Heschel believes that the experiences of Israel's prophets were extraordinary experiences of God's revelation. As such, they stand as archetypal experiences of what others may experience to a lesser extent. Even the call to be a prophet, which is but one form of revelation found in the Bible, is not totally dissimilar to the revelation experienced by others. Anyone sensitive to the divine approach may discover that she or he is being called to give prophetic witness to God. Heschel himself must have felt this intensely to write in one his poems: "I've come to sow seeing in the world— / to unveil God . . . / To wait to give the first cry: / It's becoming light!"[14]

Since Heschel regards the revelation described in the Bible as extraordinary, he tends to speak of it as unprecedented, "like no other event."[15] By this, however, he does not mean to suggest that there is no analogy between biblical revelation and other events. Indeed, his writings are replete with the conviction that the revelation of God's concern and challenge is not limited to the biblical era and may even be experienced apart from an encounter with biblical testimonies. The revelatory experience of the prophets may be unattainable to us, but it is not alien to us. We, like they, live under the divine claim that has been mediated to us through their word—but not only through their word.

In Heschel's view, the prophets' experience is to our own experience as a flame is to a spark: "Those who know that the grace of guidance may be ultimately bestowed upon those who pray for it, that in spite of their unworthiness and lowliness they may be enlightened by a spark that comes unexpectedly but in far-reaching wisdom, undeserved, yet saving, will not feel alien to the minds that perceived not a spark but a flame."[16]

Clearly, Heschel is attempting to break down resistance to the idea of the possibility of revelation as attested to in the Bible. In his judgment, resistance to revelation in the modern era is due mainly to two diametrically opposed views of human existence—that of human self-sufficiency and that of human unworthiness—and to the idea of God's absolute distance from humanity.

According to the first of these views, humanity is too great to be in need of divine guidance. Through trials and despite errors, history is a perpetual progress toward human self-redemption. In Heschel's mind, this view has been utterly discredited by the utter cruelty and destruction perpetrated by human beings throughout history, especially in the modern era.[17]

According to the second view, humanity is too insignificant in relation to the universe to warrant an address from its Creator. And considering the atrocities that human beings have committed, it is difficult to believe that humanity is either capable or worthy of receiving revelation from God. But in Heschel's view, it is precisely because human beings are so "dangerously mighty" that revelation from God is so necessary and tenable.[18]

The third view is the obverse of the second: God's absolute distance from humanity precludes a divine-human encounter. "True," Heschel replies, "it seems incredible that we should hold in our gaze words containing a breath of God. What we forget is that at this moment we breathe what God is creating."[19]

The belief that God dwells at an absolute distance from humanity involves the assumption that God is a total mystery. But from a biblical perspective, "God is *meaning beyond the mystery*,"[20] writes Heschel. "God is neither plain meaning nor just mystery. God is meaning that transcends mystery, meaning that mystery alludes to, meaning that speaks through mystery."[21] If God were a total mystery, we would be unable to attain any understanding of God. But since God is "meaning that speaks through mystery," some understanding of God is attainable.

The belief that God is a total mystery is accompanied by "the dogma of God's total silence."[22] While, as we have seen, Heschel acknowledges the silence of God, he rejects the idea of God's complete silence as antithetical to biblical faith. And he regards this faith, though not founded upon human reasoning, as a reasonable faith. If the world is God's creation, he reasons, is it not conceivable that there would be found within it revelations of God? "True, the claim of the prophets is staggering, almost incredible," admits Heschel. "But to us, living in this horribly beautiful world, God's thick silence is incomparably more staggering and totally incredible."[23]

Besides, as suggested in chapter 1, when we discern the transcendent challenge to live in harmony with the sublime mystery of existence, and when we feel the upwelling of our response to be a transcendent gift, then we know by experience and not simply by supposition that the Spirit of God has addressed and enlivened our spirit.

If God were totally silent, unable to communicate with us, then God would not truly be our God, for we human beings cannot find ultimate meaning in relation to that which is unable to relate to us. But we know God is not totally silent because, however fallibly, we know God's Word. "Out of the darkness came the voice to Moses, and out of the darkness comes the Word to us."[24]

Revelation as Mystery

Yes, it is "out of darkness," out of mystery, that the Word of God comes to us. And the Word, the revelation, even though we may discern something of its meaning, ever remains a mystery to us.

When Heschel speaks of understanding something of the meaning of God who is revealed, he realizes that God is understood as a mysterious meaning. So too he realizes that revelation is a mysterious event—"an event in the realm of the ineffable."[25]

To reveal something is to make it known. But when a mystery is made known it is not thereby erased as a mystery. When God is revealed, God's grace is more intimately felt and God's will more clearly sensed, but God's being remains a deep mystery. Likewise, when revelation is experienced, its meaning is intuited while its eventfulness remains an enigma.

In order to communicate the meaning of revelation, words are employed that in another context would be comprehensible but that in this context suggest the incomprehensible. The same words may be used in either a descriptive or an indicative way. When used to communicate the meaning of revelation, otherwise descriptive words are used to indicate the indescribable. Heschel offers the following example: "'And God said: Let there be light' is different in spirit from a statement such as 'And Smith said: Let us turn on the light.' The second statement conveys a definite meaning; the first statement evokes an inner response to an ineffable meaning."[26] In light of this example, it is clear why Heschel maintains that "the surest way of misunderstanding revelation is to take it literally" or that "the cardinal sin in thinking about ultimate issues is *literal-mindedness*."[27]

Literal-mindedness is the failure to discern the unique connotations that otherwise descriptive terms assume when used indicatively in a religious context. Words about God or revelation are intimations rather than definitions, allusions rather than descriptions. "When taken literally, they either turn flat, narrow and shallow or become ventriloquistic myths. For example, the dogma of creation has often been reduced to a tale and robbed of its authentic meaning; but as an allusion to ultimate mystery it is of inexhaustible relevance."[28]

But while words used to speak of revelation—words such as the biblical expression "God said"—must not be taken literally, neither should they be regarded as simply figurative words, if by this it is meant that God does not in some real sense address human beings. In Heschel's view, God really does address humanity, even if the address is not perceptible to our bodily senses. "It is not only by their ears that human beings can hear. It is not only the physical sound that can reach the human spirit."[29]

God's "voice" transcends human voices and is inaudible to human ears, but it reaches the human spirit. This being so, "the speech of God is not less but more than literally real."[30] The expression "God said" is not a hyperbole; it is an understatement.

Since words concerning divine revelation should not be taken either literally or figuratively, they should be understood as "indicative words [that] must be taken responsively . . . not [as] portraits but *clues*, serving as guides, suggesting a line of thinking."[31] We will understand the meaning of a biblical term like "God said" when, responding to the biblical message, we are open to the impact of God's concern and challenge. As a mystery, revelation is an event that cannot be proved rationally but can be understood existentially. And this existential understanding renders a greater assurance of the credibility of revelation than could any rational proof. Like an expression of human love, divine revelation—which is, ultimately, the revelation of love—is a mysterious event filled with meaning that can only be understood by responding to it.

Revelation in and through the Bible

Since in the Jewish tradition the Bible is regarded as a collection of inspired responses to divine revelation, Heschel, like many other Jews, believes that the presence of God can be found in its pages. Responsiveness to the Bible may therefore be a pathway to faith in God. In particular, since the Bible is the foundational document on which the Jewish tradition was formed, responsiveness to the Bible is an essential feature of any authentically Jewish approach to God.

Responsiveness to the Bible

While a sense for the presence of God in the Bible may elicit responsiveness to it, Heschel suggests that by responding to the Bible—whether or not we initially sense God's presence in it—we may come to discern that presence in and through its words.

It is not simply by reading the words of the Bible but by heeding its principal teachings that God's presence may be found within it. "We cannot sense God's presence in the Bible except by being responsive to it," writes Heschel. "Only living with its words, only sympathy with its pathos, will open our ear to its voice."[32] But, we may ask, why respond to the Bible if God's presence in it is not sensed in the first place?

Even if we cannot sense God's presence in the Bible except by being responsive to it, we must sense something important in it before deciding to give it our sustained attention. Perhaps the claims made on behalf of the Bible by exemplars of holiness entice us to investigate the Bible's claims made on behalf of God. Since the Bible "is the fountainhead of the finest human strivings in the Western World," and because it "has given birth and shape to a myriad of precious things in the lives of individuals and peoples,"[33] it deserves our responsiveness even if we are not convinced that God may be found within it.

Perhaps our own spiritual hunger prompts us to try living in accord with a message that has nourished millions of other people. Maybe the suspicion that the Bible contains a message that can flood our lives with meaning stirs us to respond to its central claims and thereby come to sense the reality of God in those claims. We may sense God's presence in the Bible only by responding to the Bible, but we may first respond to the Bible because we sense, or at least suspect, that it contains a message, and perhaps even a presence, that deserves our response.

But what, then, might Heschel mean when he claims that "to sense the presence of God in the Bible, one must learn *to be present* to God in the Bible"?[34] What would move us "*to be present* to God in the Bible" if we did not in the first place sense the presence in it?

Might we interpret Heschel to mean that by responding to the biblical message, even prior to sensing the divine presence in it, we are in effect being present to God, even if unaware of God's presence? In human relationships, is it true that a person can be present to another only when the other is perceived as present? Or is there a sense in which someone might be present to another simply by longing for the other's presence? Prior to the statement of Heschel's we are currently considering, he writes: "To be able to encounter the spirit within the words, we must learn to crave for an affinity with the pathos of God."[35] If "to encounter the spirit" is synonymous with "to sense the presence," then "to crave for an affinity" may be the same as "to be present." If this is true, then we may be present to God prior to sensing God's presence simply by craving an affinity with God—and this we may do either explicitly or implicitly, consciously or unconsciously.

The Sense of God's Presence in the Bible

But the question remains, how may we come to sense and accept the presence of God in the Bible?

To be responsive to the Bible includes heeding the grandeur of its message and its appeal to conscience. Could such an appeal to the core of our personhood come from a source not itself personal? In responding to biblical words that speak to our hearts, we come to sense the personal source of those words. Is that source merely human? Are the prophets of Israel, for example, the sole personal sources of the words they speak? Those who live with the words of the Bible feel kinship with Isaiah, Jeremiah, and other prophets. But the words these prophets utter contain a glory and a challenge that the prophets themselves claim not to have authored and to which they themselves must submit.

"The light with which a prophet is aglow casts into the shade his own powers of vision and self-awareness."[36] This is why prophetic words are often prefaced or concluded with "Thus says the Lord." This is also why those who are inspired and challenged by prophetic words believe them to convey a divine presence. Such words are too heartrending and healing to be of human origin alone. The personal source of those words is too life-giving and demanding to be no more than human. The light with which the prophets are aglow casts not only their self-awareness into the shade but also the awareness of them by those whom they address.

Whatever kinship may be felt with the prophets, those who respond to them become more aware of the light with which the prophets are aglow than of the prophets themselves. No matter how close the presence of the prophets may be, it is the transcendent presence to which they bear witness that is felt more intimately. The personal presence or light conveyed through prophetic words is so overwhelming and empowering that it can be nothing other than divine. God is the presence encountered in biblical words, a presence known to transcend the prophets since they too must submit to its claim while at the same time being set aglow by its light.

In light of what has been said about how we come to sense and accept the presence of God in the Bible, it should be clear that such acceptance, while not the result of reasoning, is nonetheless compatible with reason. Is it not reasonable to accept as divinely inspired a message that presents itself as a claim that confronts the prophets as well as those whom they confront with it? And is it not reasonable to accept as divinely inspired that which impassions and empowers human beings to seek justice, to love mercy, and to live in holiness? And if it is reasonable to accept the presence of God in the Bible, is it not reasonable as well to believe in the origin of the Bible in God?

Divine and Human Authorship of the Bible

"More decisive than *the origin of the Bible in God* is *the presence of God in the Bible*. It is the sense for the presence that leads us to a belief in its origin."[37] When the presence of God is encountered in the Bible it becomes possible to believe that God inspired the Bible into being. It is not a matter of proving the divine origin of the Bible but of recognizing that the ultimate source of a message filled with divine presence must also be divine. "God" is the name for the power that created the world and inspired the Word.

This does not mean that God is the sole author of the Bible and that the human writers are no more than scribes. It only means that God is the primary source of inspiration for the biblical writers, that "the Bible reflects its divine as well as human authorship."[38]

According to Heschel, there are in the Bible words of human beings inspired by God and words that are not. Concerning the former, God's revelation and the inspired human responses to it are expressed in human words, according to how human beings, no matter how inspired by God, perceive and respond to the revelation. Concerning the latter, the Bible records acts and words that obviously are not meant to be taken as God's Word—blasphemous tirades, rebellious deeds, etc.—and thus "it is incorrect to maintain that all words in the Bible originated in the spirit of God."[39]

No one hears the Word of God as it is. God addresses every person according to her or his ability to understand the address.[40] Even the understanding of the prophets does not reflect the divine perspective as it is. "The words of Scripture are the only lasting record of what was conveyed to the prophets. At the same time they are neither identical with, nor the eternally adequate rendering of, divine wisdom."[41] "Prophecy is superior to human wisdom, and God's love is superior to prophecy."[42]

Moreover, not all of the prophets' claims made on behalf of God appear to be equally inspired, and some are "incompatible with our certainty of the compassion of God."[43] Thus, keeping in mind that "the standards by which those passages are criticized are impressed upon us by the Bible," Heschel asserts that "in the name of God's mercy, we . . . have the right to challenge the harsh statements of the prophets."[44]

The Central Idea of the Bible's Prophetic Theology

The fact that some of the prophets' statements are "incompatible with our certainty of the compassion of God" means that these statements are incompatible with what Heschel calls "*the* central idea in prophetic theology," that is, "the idea of *pathos*,"[45] which, throughout his writings, he repeatedly associates with compassion. "Pathos, concern for the world, is the very ethos of God," writes Heschel. "This ethical sensitivity of God . . . is reflected in the prophets' declarations."[46] Where this sensitivity is not reflected in their declarations, the prophets are off message as prophets of the God whose "own nature" is expressed in "being compassionate."[47]

"The divine pathos embraces all life, past, present, and future. . . . It is a concern that has the attribute of eternity, transcending all history, as well as the attribute of universality, embracing all nations, encompassing animals as well as human beings."[48] Nevertheless, the expressions of pathos are historical; otherwise they would not signify God's involvement with historical beings.

The very fact that we human beings are historical creatures means that God's involvement with us must be historical, entailing a dynamic relationship in which there is call and response on both sides. Since God is truly involved in our lives, God relates to us according to where we are and what we are feeling, thinking, willing, and doing. This means that, even though God's loving concern for us is eternal, God's attitudes and actions in relation to us are subject to change as we human beings change in relation to God, to each other, and to the world. Thus it is that whatever we do affects not only our own lives but also the life of God insofar as it is directed to us.[49] And this is so even to the point of suffering.

Heschel interprets the prophets of Israel as suggesting that "God does not stand outside the range of human suffering and sorrow."[50] Human history is to a large extent a record of human misery, and since God is concerned for human beings and involved in their history, God must be affected by human suffering. "God's participation in human history . . . finds its deepest expression in the fact that God can actually suffer."[51]

The anguish of God echoes throughout the Bible. By way of example, Heschel comments on Isaiah 42:14 by pointing out that the allusion to God as "a woman in travail" conveys not only a sense of urgency to God's action but also a sense of the deep intensity of God's suffering. Heschel also reminds us that "of God's involvement in human suffering the prophet declares courageously: '*In all their affliction He was afflicted*'" (Isa 63:9).[52]

Heschel would surely concur with one of the most famous comments by Alfred North Whitehead, the patriarch of modern process philosophy: "God is the great companion—the fellow-sufferer who understands."[53] Pathos is concern unto suffering, and God's concern is full of pathos.

This idea of divine pathos, that God suffers out of compassion for God's creatures, is directly opposed to the classical metaphysical theology inspired by Greek philosophy. Yet Heschel believes this idea accords with the biblical understanding of God and renders a more accurate theological interpretation of traditional Jewish piety than does the classical doctrine of God's impassibility, the idea that God is incapable of suffering.

It is because of its being steeped in Greek philosophical approaches to reality that classical metaphysical theology opposes the idea of divine pathos. "The static idea of divinity is the outcome of two strands of thought: the ontological notion of stability and the psychological view of the emotions as disturbances of the soul."[54] Heschel examines each of these strands of thought, shows their incompatibility with the biblical understanding of God, and advances the idea of divine pathos as a more plausible view of ultimate reality.

Concerning ontology, Heschel points to the formidable influence of Parmenides of Elea on later philosophical theology. According to Parmenides, being is immovable and movement is illusory. Although later Greek philosophy recognized the reality of change, as stressed by Heraclitus, it tended to restrict Heraclitus's theory to the world of sense perception. Classical metaphysical theology applied Parmenides' concept of unchangeable being to God, affirming a Greek philosophical assumption that change implies an imperfection that is incompatible with divine being. Heschel responds to the ontology of Parmenides' Eleatic school and to the metaphysical theology based on it as follows: "If we think of being as something beyond and detached from beings, we may well arrive at an Eleatic notion. An ontology, however, concerned with being as involved in all beings or as the source of all beings will find it impossible to separate being from action or movement, and thus postulate a dynamic concept of divine Being."[55]

Again we may note a parallel between Heschel's thought and that of Alfred North Whitehead. Although he never addresses the question of an affinity between Whitehead's process philosophy and his own biblical philosophy, it seems clear that, whatever differences there may be between the two, Heschel would be able to endorse one of Whitehead's central tenets: "God is not to be treated as an exception to all metaphysical principles" but as "their chief exemplification."[56]

Viewing God as dynamic, as self-moving in relation to the world and as moved by beings in the world, Heschel believes not only that God is involved in history but that there is "history in God."[57] This does not mean he thinks of God's nature or essence as changeable but that God's modes of being in relation to the world may change.

One reason that classical metaphysical theology refuses to acknowledge divine change is that God is viewed as perfect, and change is thought to imply imperfection. Why change, so it is thought, unless one's present state of being is less than perfect? According to classical theism, God is by definition the perfect being. And being is defined as pure actuality; it therefore admits of no potentiality. Potential indicates the capacity to be affected and thereby to experience change. But God, being perfect, need not—indeed, cannot—change.

According to this definition of perfection, it must be admitted that the God of biblical faith is not perfect, for this God has not actualized all the expressions of divine concern that are to be actualized. But the Bible is not concerned with the kind of perfection defined by classical theistic philosophy. From a biblical perspective, pure actuality is no synonym for divine perfection. God suffers change not because of any imperfection but because different situations demand different divine replies.

Nowhere does Heschel suggest that God ever changes for the better, that movement or history in God implies that God is in the process of becoming more divine. God has the potential to be affected and to enact responses not yet actual, but this does not mean that God is thereby perfected. We may move God because God allows us to, but we must not assume that by doing so we somehow enhance God's divinity. There is history in God not because of a divine imperfection but because God is perfectly responsive to the changes in history.

The second strand of thought that Heschel cites as a source of the static idea of divinity is, as noted, "the psychological view of the emotions as disturbances of the soul." Classical thinkers like Maimonides or Thomas Aquinas, unlike Aristotle from whom they derive philosophical inspiration, do not deny God's concern for creation. They simply deny that God is concerned to the point of being affected by creation. Yet to have concern for creatures while remaining unaffected by their actions, unmoved by their plight, would be to have a rather remote concern, if concern at all it be. Whatever can be said of such an attitude, it does not signify the existence of a real relationship—as Aquinas admits in saying that "in God there is no real relation to creatures, but we speak about God as related inasmuch as creatures are referred to Him."[58] Heschel's view is the polar opposite: God has "a passionate relationship" with creatures and "a feeling of intimate concern" for them.[59]

Just as the Greek philosophy adopted by classical theism regards change as an imperfection, so does it consider passion or pathos, which is an affection implying change, as a sign of weakness. Self-sufficiency is a presupposed ideal of this philosophy, and human dignity is "seen in the activity of the mind, in acts of self-determination."[60] Since pathos is aroused by something outside the self, and since it is considered to be an emotional reaction rather than an intellectual act, it is viewed as an imperfection.

In genuine Hebraic thinking, on the contrary, self-sufficiency in the sense of the self being unaffected by realities outside the self is no ideal. In fact, within the biblical tradition, the moral ideal is precisely the opposite of the Greek ideal of self-sufficiency, and one of Heschel's interpreters points out that this biblical ideal is confirmed by modern psychiatry: "Psychiatry provides mounting evidence that the healthy personality is open and vulnerable, willing to take risks and able to bear the hurt. This describes the biblical God *par excellence*. . . . It is just possible that our resistance to the idea of divine pathos . . . is in fact a rationalization. It may be motivated by the fear of taking the same risks that God takes."[61]

Understandably, resistance to the idea of pathos has its roots in a philosophical system in which reason is disconnected from emotion and preferred over it. It was this disconnection and preference "that enabled Greek philosophy to exclude all emotion from the nature of Deity, while at the same time ascribing thought and contemplation to it."[62] This dissociation of reason from emotion is alien to biblical thinking, as is the disparagement of emotion. In fact, says Heschel: "Thought is part of emotion. We think because we are moved. . . . Emotion may be defined as the consciousness of being moved."[63] Moreover, in a biblical perspective, emotion is indispensable to the life of action: "Great deeds are done by those who are filled with *ruaḥ*, with pathos."[64]

Given this positive appreciation of emotion in the Bible, "there was no reason to shun the idea of pathos in the understanding of God."[65] Divine pathos, though an emotional response, is "understood not as an unreasoned emotion, but as an act formed with intention, depending on free will, the result of decision and determination."[66] Acts of passion can be devoid of reasoned purpose but they need not be; "emotion can be reasonable just as reason can be emotional."[67] The divine pathos is God's reason and will charged with passion, or it is God's passion informed by reason and will.

Moreover, since "God is the source of justice," Heschel claims that God's "pathos is ethical";[68] it is a passion for justice. But this does not mean that divine pathos is concerned with "strict justice." God's pathos never disregards the standards of justice, and "the concern for justice is an act of love," but "beyond all justice is God's compassion."[69] In short, for Heschel, "God's pathos is compassion."[70]

Clearly, Heschel believes that the idea of divine pathos is both religiously important and philosophically credible, superior to the idea of an impersonal, disengaged deity. A god unaffected by human concerns and cries, unmoved by the plight of creatures, would be religiously irrelevant to us. And such a god would be both ontologically and psychologically inferior to us, since we human beings are able to respond to the concerns and cries of each other, and also to the plight of other creatures. What in this regard we human beings may do humanly, the God of biblical revelation does divinely, supremely. Such a God alone is worthy of our worship, worthy to be called God.

And this is so even if the God of biblical revelation is not viewed as omnipotent. Associated with Heschel's view of God's pathos is his contention that "the idea of divine omnipotence . . . is a non-Jewish idea."[71] Thus, he suggests, God's presence in history should not be understood as

God's dominance of history.[72] "To regard all that happens as the workings of Providence is to deny human responsibility,"[73] as it is also to deny the love of God. "God's mercy is too great to permit the innocent to suffer," says Heschel. "But there are forces that interfere with God's mercy, with God's power."[74]

Given that Heschel says, "God's mercy is too great to permit the innocent to suffer," his claim that "there are forces that interfere with God's mercy" obviously should not be interpreted to mean that God's mercy is limited but that forces at work in the world sometimes prevent God's mercy from preventing the suffering of the innocent. What he intends to suggest here is what he explicitly states in various contexts, that the power of God is limited, rendering the unlimited divine mercy less effective than God desires. "Between mercy and power," writes Heschel, "mercy takes precedence—and to the mercy of Heaven there is no limit!"[75]

Heschel's rejection of the idea of divine omnipotence is rooted in his interpretation of the prophets of Israel as emphasizing the pathos of God rather than the power of God: "In the interpretation of religion it is generally assumed that God is, above all, 'the name for some experience of power.' . . . Such interpretation, valid as it may be for the understanding of other types of religion, hardly applies to the prophets. Here the reality of the divine is sensed as pathos rather than as power, and the most exalted idea applied to God is not infinite wisdom, infinite power, but infinite concern."[76]

In the prophetic vision, according to Heschel, "the grandeur and majesty of God do not come to expression in the display of ultimate sovereignty and power, but rather in rendering righteousness and mercy."[77] And, as we will discuss in the final section of the next chapter, God needs human cooperation for the righteousness and mercy of God to be displayed in this world.[78] Out of deeply felt sympathy for the pathos of God, the prophets of Israel exemplify and champion this human cooperation, not passively relying on some imagined divine omnipotence but laboring with God in the divine-human cause of redemption.[79]

So, in Heschel's view, although not every word of the Bible is inspired by God, and although some of its declarations are even incompatible with the compassion of God, responsiveness to the Bible is nonetheless a pathway to faith in God because the Bible communicates the Word, and even the presence, of this God of pathos who is the source of all compassion by which the world is redeemed.

Revelation as Torah—In and Beyond the Bible

Another name for God's revelation to the Jewish people is "Torah," and this is why Judaism is often referred to as "the Way of Torah." In the strictest sense of the term, "Torah" designates the first five books of the Bible. More broadly, it refers to the Jewish Bible as a whole. And even more broadly, it refers to the entire corpus of authoritative Jewish religious writings, especially but not exclusively the Bible and the Talmud. So a discussion of God's revelation to the Jewish people needs to include consideration of Torah beyond the Bible.

Judaism as More than a Biblical Religion

While Jewish faith necessarily involves responsiveness to the Bible, Heschel reminds us that "Judaism is not purely a biblical religion."[80] "The concern for God continued throughout the ages, and in order to understand Judaism we must inquire about the way and the spirit of that concern in post-biblical Jewish history as well."[81] The way and the spirit of Jewish concern for God, the way of Torah, is epitomized in the rabbinic literature—especially as compiled in the Talmud—of early post-biblical Judaism.

"As a report about revelation, the Bible itself is *a midrash*"[82] (that is, a commentary or an interpretation). But since "the full meaning of the biblical words was not disclosed once and for all,"[83] this great midrash (or collection of *midrashim*, interpretations) stands in need of subsequent midrashim. Thus, revelation and the Bible that conveys it are not the only wellsprings of the way of Torah. In fact, says Heschel, "Judaism is based upon a minimum of revelation and a maximum of interpretation, upon the will of God and upon the understanding of Israel."[84] Likewise, "the Bible is not an end but a beginning,"[85] the beginning of a heritage that is only presaged in the Bible.

"The Bible is the seed, God is the sun, but we are the soil. Every generation is expected to bring forth new understanding and new realization."[86] While this contribution is expected of every generation, it is especially the sages of each generation that convey and provoke the genuine understanding and realization of Jewish faith. Moreover, to attain this, the Jewish people and its latter-day sages must pay special attention to the interpretations of the rabbinic sages of those generations, particularly from the second to the sixth centuries CE, that created the rabbinic tradition. "We approach the laws of the Bible through the interpretations and wisdom of the Rabbis. . . . The prophets' inspirations and the sages' interpretations are equally important. The savants are heirs to the prophets; they determine and interpret the meaning of the word. There is much liberty and much power in the insights of the sages: they have the power to set aside a precept of the Torah when conditions require it."[87]

It is important to stress the fact that the Bible is approached through the interpretations of the sages precisely in order "to bring forth new understanding and new realization" in our own day, not simply to reiterate the ancient interpretations. "The prophets make us partners of an existence meant for us. What was revealed to them was not for their sake but intended to inspire us. . . . To disregard the importance of *continuous understanding* is an evasion of the living challenge of the prophets . . . a denial of the deeper meaning of 'the oral Torah.' . . . For the Torah is an invitation to perceptivity, a call for *continuous understanding*."[88]

So just as "we must become aware of the obscurantism of mechanical deference to the Bible,"[89] so too must we be aware of this attitude in relation to rabbinic writings. The fact that the sages "determine and interpret the meaning of the word" does not mean that new meanings can no longer be determined, new interpretations advanced. On the contrary, this is precisely what is required in order for each generation "to bring forth new understanding and new realization," or to realize "*continuous understanding*."

"To have faith does not mean . . . to dwell in the shadow of old ideas conceived by prophets and sages, to live off an inherited estate of doctrines and dogmas. . . . Authentic faith is more than the echo of a tradition. It is a creative situation, an event."[90] Obviously, for Heschel, this does not mean that authentic Jewish faith in no way echoes a tradition, but when it does it must lend its own unique tone to that tradition. It involves the correlation of the witness of tradition and new encounters with God that the tradition may have fostered but did not previously include. Authentic Jewish faith indeed does reaffirm some of the "old ideas conceived by prophets and sages," but it does not merely "live off" these ideas. Rather, while bearing witness to traditional ideas that illumine present situations, authentic Jewish faith also testifies to the impact of God's presence in the present and to credible ideas that emerge in the wake of that impact. In short, authentic Jewish faith bears witness to what God has revealed and to what God is revealing.

Judaism as the Way of Torah

And what God reveals as Torah has to do with a lot more than what many people think of when they hear the word "Torah," that is, divine law. There are two senses in which Heschel thinks it is inappropriate to limit the word "Torah" to law or to a system of laws.

In the first place, "the Torah is primarily *divine ways* rather than *divine laws.*"[91] By this Heschel means that the Torah not only contains divine laws by which human beings must live in relation to God but also represents the ways by which God relates to human beings. Heschel reminds us that Moses prayed "Let me know Thy ways" (Exod 33:13) and that what God asks of us is summarized as "to walk in all God's ways" (Deut 10:12).[92]

A second reason why Heschel views the Torah as more than law is that only a portion of the Torah deals with legal matters. The Torah contains both *halacha* (Jewish law) and *agada* (Jewish lore), whether it is understood in its narrowest sense as the first five books of the Bible, or as the entire Hebrew Bible, or in its broadest sense as both Bible and subsequent authoritative Jewish religious texts.

Judaism is "the way of Torah." So if Torah is reduced to halacha, Judaism becomes merely the way of halacha, a religion of law. Such "pan-halachism," as Heschel calls it, is a misrepresentation of Judaism. "Those who would restrict Judaism to *Halacha* will distort its image and deprive it of its grandeur."[93]

Love is the supreme principle of Jewish law: "All observance is training in the art of love."[94] And since genuine love involves the heart and the soul of the lover, the law of love cannot be fulfilled by mere external compliance with the law. But those who reduce Torah and Judaism to halacha tend also to reduce halacha to external conformity to the law.

Heschel is critical of pan-halachism because of his love for halacha. "The observance of the law is the richest source of religious experience," but pan-halachism spells the demise of genuine halachic living because "halacha is ultimately dependent upon agada."[95] Agada is the inspiration behind halacha. The heart of the law is love of God and neighbor, but it is not the law itself but rather agada that motivates such love.

Agada and halacha are both essential components of the Torah, and their interrelationship is the essence of Judaism. Agada tells of the sublime mystery of creation, the marvel of the divine-human covenant, and the joy of human relationships within the covenant. Narrating the love story between God and the Jewish people, agada sets the soul aflame and rouses the thirst for God and for a life compatible with God's love. Agada thus inspires love for halacha, for God's law; it teaches that the law of God was given as a sign of divine love, that enacting the law is not for its own sake but for the sake of honoring God and ennobling humanity, that the law therefore is not meant as a burden with which to comply but a helpmate to cherish and embrace.

A related issue that Heschel addresses is whether and to what extent the Torah's laws are the will of God. "We believe that there is a law, the essence of which is derived from prophetic events, and the interpretation of which is in the hands of the sages."[96] In saying that *the essence* of the law is derived from prophetic events, does Heschel mean to suggest that it is *only* the essence of the law that is derived from revelation? If so, what does he mean by the essence of the law? Does he mean, for example, primary ethical commandments to love neighbors and strangers as we love ourselves (Lev 19:18 and 19:34)?

The closest Heschel comes to saying explicitly whether or not he believes that all the laws of halacha (whether still binding or not) are the result of revelation is the following statement: "There are times in Jewish history when the main issue is not what parts of the law cannot be fulfilled but what parts of the law can be and ought to be fulfilled, fulfilled as law, as an expression and interpretation of the will of God."[97] From his own writings, it seems this is also an issue for Heschel: what parts of the law ought to be regarded and fulfilled as an expression of the will of God?

Certainly Heschel rejects the view that there is "no distinction between the eternal and the temporal," and he points out that some of the laws of the Torah, such as found in Exodus 21, do not represent ideals but compromises, realistic attempts to refine the moral condition of people in biblical times.[98] Since, as previously noted, Heschel claims that, in the name of God's mercy, we have the right to challenge statements of the prophets, no doubt he would affirm the right to challenge some of the laws of halacha, whether of prophetic or rabbinic origin. In fact, paraphrasing the medieval sage Rashi, Heschel claims: "Sometimes one should annul parts of the Torah to act for the Lord."[99] But just as the standards used to criticize certain statements of the prophets come from the Bible, so too the standards used to criticize some halachic laws are derived from the Torah. If some laws are deemed no longer binding it is precisely because they are no longer deemed compatible with the forever binding essentials of the Torah's halacha.

But even if all halachic laws are not derived from revelation or required of those within the Jewish covenant with God, Heschel believes that God may expect observance of not only the central ethical commands of the Torah like love of neighbors and strangers but also of the ritual laws having to do with "the days of the week, the food that we eat, the holidays of the year," which he includes among "the frontiers of faith."[100] "Faith . . . cannot rest content with essences. Faith knows no boundaries between the will of God and all of life."[101]

"If we are ready to believe that it is God who requires us 'to love kindness,' is it more difficult to believe that God requires us to hallow the Sabbath and not to violate its sanctity?" asks Heschel.[102] "Scientists dedicate their lives to the study of the habits of insects or the properties of plants. To them every trifle is significant. . . . Just as the self-sacrificing devotion of the scientist seems torture to the debauchee, so the poetry of [religious] rigorism jars on the ears of the cynic. But, perhaps, the question of what benediction to pronounce upon a certain type of food, the problem of matching the material with the spiritual, is more important than is generally imagined."[103]

"It is primarily in the way in which we gratify physical needs that the seed of holiness is planted. . . . Judaism teaches us how even the gratification of animal needs can be an act of sanctification. The enjoyment of food may be a way of purification. Something of my soul may be drowned in a glass of water, when its content is gulped down as if nothing in the world mattered except my thirst. But we can come a bit closer to God when remembering Him still more in excitement and passion."[104] If this is true, might it not be that God wills and asks not only for ethical deeds but ritual ones as well?

Love is the essence and purpose of the Torah and its halacha, and, as has been noted, "all observance is training in the art of love." Thus, claims Heschel, "to forget that love is the purpose of all *mitsvot* [commandments; good deeds] is to vitiate their meaning."[105] Affixing a mezuzah to the doorpost of a home, praying at prescribed hours, wearing the prayer shawl, abstaining from certain foods and koshering others, lighting Sabbath candles, each of these is meant as an act of love.

True, people can love without performing such deeds, but these are reminders of the duty to love and are themselves ways of expressing love. "All mitsvot are means of evoking in us the awareness of living in the neighborhood of God."[106] And when such awareness is abiding, love of God and God's creation may likewise abide and be enhanced. Is it so difficult to believe, then, that God expects not only love but also certain ways of expressing love as distinct reminders of our living in the presence of God?

But regardless of the extent to which the Torah's laws reflect the will of God, Heschel believes that the Torah "carries the presence of God."[107] Because some Jews not only affirm this—the Torah as a vehicle of God's presence—but also perhaps use "imagery describing the Torah [that] is too exalting and consequently excessively audacious," Heschel suggests that there is a "danger of making the Torah a substitute for God."[108] But, reminding us that within the Jewish tradition "again and again we are admonished against taking a totalitarian view of the Torah," Heschel claims that "the Torah is not an end in itself; it is transcended by God."[109]

If some Jews are tempted "to understand the Torah not only as possessing a divine quality, as being saturated with divinity, but as being divinity itself," it is because they "assert a close identity between the Torah and God's wisdom."[110] But Heschel claims that, according to the rabbinic tradition, "the Torah in our hands is some of God's wisdom," not all of it.[111] The Torah is to be studied, observed, and cherished; God alone is to be adored. Yet since the Torah conveys the wisdom and the presence of God, love for the Torah is an expression of love for God, faith in God.

CHAPTER THREE

JEWISH RESPONSES TO GOD

"The main aspects of religious existence" within the Jewish tradition, Heschel reminds us, are "worship, learning, and action,"[1] and much of his writing is devoted to elucidating these as responses to God.

Worship

"Praise is our first response" to the presence of God, says Heschel. Unable to describe that presence, "we can only sing, we can only utter words of adoration."[2] But, as indicated in chapter 1, Heschel suggests that to discern the presence of God we must be sensitive to the sublime mystery of nature and humanity. He regards wonder and awe as the appropriate human responses to the sublime mystery and, as such, prerequisites of praise. It is appropriate, then, that we discuss Heschel's understanding of wonder and awe before considering his approach to worship.

Wonder and Awe

"What seems to be natural is wondrous."[3] And wonder is the natural human response to the wondrous, which is another name for the sublime dimension of reality. Since the sublime alludes to the divine, wonder nurtures worship as a response to the divine. "The way to prayer leads through *acts of wonder*."[4]

While the sublime invites wonder, its presence does not guarantee the emergence of wonder, which is both a gift and a response. There are times when, unprepared, we are overcome with wonder, yet it is up to us to "keep alive the sense of wonder through deeds of wonder."[5] The sublime marvel of nature and of neighbors is unveiled to us when we approach them with reverence. Wonder seizes us when we take nothing and no one for granted, when we take the time to treat things and persons as precious and unique.

Accordingly, Heschel speaks of "a will to wonder,"[6] and he contrasts the way of living by wonder with the way of expediency: "We go out to meet the world not only by way of expediency but also by way of wonder. In the first we accumulate information in order to dominate; in the second we deepen our appreciation in order to respond."[7] Heschel conveys this same idea when he contrasts the way of appreciation with the way of manipulation as two primary ways in which we relate ourselves to the world. In the latter we see in what surrounds us "things to be handled, forces to be managed, objects to be put to use," while in the former we see "things to be acknowledged, understood, valued, or admired."[8]

Thus, the will to wonder is the resolve to face reality with appreciation, and living by way of wonder involves living with an attitude of appreciation. There are appropriate ways of manipulating nature's forces, as there are also harmful ways. To avoid the latter we need to cultivate an appreciation for nature's beauty and grandeur, not only for its power or energy. Such appreciation leads to wonder and reflects it.

Just as the way of wonder is opposed to ways of expediency and manipulation, it is also contrary to the attitude of merely accepting things at face value. "Wonder, or radical amazement, is a way of going beyond what is given in thing and thought, refusing to take anything for granted, to regard anything as final. It is our honest response to the grandeur and mystery of reality, our confrontation with that which transcends the given."[9]

Since we *confront* what "transcends the given" rather than simply *infer* it from "what is given in thing and thought," Heschel even says that "the indication of what transcends all things is given to us with the same immediacy as the things themselves."[10] But if our attitude is one that merely accepts the apparent, we will fail to discern the indication of transcendence.

To sense the beyond in the evident, the transcendent meaning of natural objects, we must live in a spirit of wonder, in a state of mind that takes nothing for granted: "Spiritually we cannot live by merely reiterating borrowed or inherited knowledge. Inquire of your soul, what does it know, what does it take for granted. It will tell you only no-thing is taken for granted; each thing is a surprise, *being is unbelievable*. We are amazed at seeing anything at all; amazed not only at particular values and things but *at the unexpectedness of being as such*, at the fact there is being at all."[11]

When we refuse to take the world for granted, to merely accept the apparent, and when, instead, we attempt to face the world as if for the first time, then we may understand what Heschel means when he writes: "The world is not just here. It shocks us into amazement."[12]

Clearly, the wonder of which Heschel speaks goes beyond the level of intellectual curiosity, which though a step beyond mere acceptance of the apparent is not a matter of being stunned "at the unexpectedness of being as such." The wonder he describes as "radical amazement" is an "ultimate wonder" that surpasses the "rational wonder" of curiosity. Questions born of curiosity drive us to investigate how things in the world function and relate, but wonder's question of why there is a world is "*a question of amazement*, not of curiosity,"[13] and it drives us to look beyond the world for an answer to it. "The world is a mystery, a question, not an answer" and, therefore, "the most pressing problem is, what does it stand for? What is its meaning?"[14]

When, in a state of wonder, we sense that the world is a question, not an answer, we are overcome by the realization that nature has not endowed itself with its own grandeur, nor have we endowed the world with the meaning to which it alludes. In such a situation we cannot circumvent the supreme question, "Who is the great author? Why is there a world at all?"[15]

In wonder we come to realize that the great miracle of life is something we witness and generate rather than something we ourselves create, and this realization may prompt us to believe that the God to whom biblical religion bears witness is the great author of life and the transcendent meaning of the world. Wonder is, therefore, the soil in which worship of God is rooted, and it is the climate in which worship thrives.

But wonder is not the only prerequisite of worship. In moments of wonder, when we sense the sublime dimension of existence, it is upon mystery that we come and in reverence that we stand. Life's grandeur directs our attention to its mystery, and our wonder is filled with awe.

Although Heschel does not state it explicitly, there are two levels of awe discernable in his writings: awe as a *response to mystery* and awe as a *response to God*. Since God is a mystery, awe of God includes awe of mystery. But because not all mystery is divine, it is possible to feel awe in the face of non-divine reality without an explicit awe of God. Nevertheless, since life's mystery evokes an attitude of awe in which the question of God is raised and is the setting in which the presence of God is disclosed, awe in response to the mystery of created reality often gives way to awe of God.

The Hebrew word *yirah* has two meanings: fear and awe. Heschel makes a clear distinction between them: "Awe, unlike fear, does not make us shrink from the awe-inspiring object, but, on the contrary, draws us near to it. This is why awe is compatible with both love and joy. In a sense, awe is the antithesis of fear. To feel 'The Lord is my light and my salvation' is to feel 'Whom shall I fear?' (Psalms 27:1)."[16]

Heschel would agree with Rudolf Otto's celebrated depiction of the *mysterium* as at once both *tremendum* and *fascinosum*, overwhelming and fascinating.[17] Therefore, although Heschel says that awe is "in a sense" the antithesis of fear because it "draws us near to" the awe-inspiring object, he does not reduce awe to fascination alone. A feeling of what Otto calls *tremor* is, for Heschel, also an aspect of awe; not a tremor that "makes us shrink from" the awesome but that humbles us in its presence.

In awe we are drawn toward the mystery in response to which we are diffident and devout. Awe includes both attraction and veneration, rapture and reserve; it is a yearning love for the divine in whose presence we shudder with adoration. Awe may supersede fear, but it does not remove our blush in the presence of the holy. The type of fear that is the antithesis of awe is that which fills us with horror and despair. But if by "fear" is meant the state of being struck still by life's mystery, silenced by God's presence, then in this sense fear is not the antithesis of awe but an aspect of it.

It is important to realize that awe includes both fascination and tremor. Fascination without tremor would result in familiarity without esteem; tremor apart from fascination would be sheer dread. Religious awe in Heschel's sense is not dread; nor is it mere familiarity. Rather, it is both captivation and respect, intimacy and esteem. This is why Heschel uses the word "reverence" as a synonym for "awe."

According to Heschel, awe is not simply a significant experience; it is a "*categorical imperative*" for human beings to cultivate a sense of awe.[18] Reality, abounding in mystery, demands such a response. Just as wonder is the appropriate human response to what is wondrous, awe is the only fitting reply to what is awesome or mysterious. Moreover, awe in response to the mystery of being is imperative because its lack leads to the destruction of being. "Forfeit your sense of awe, let your conceit diminish your ability to revere, and the universe becomes a market place for you."[19]

Awe, or reverence, is a categorical imperative because it is a prerequisite of ethical living, which is a prerequisite for the survival of humanity. Where reverence for life abounds, so do justice and peace. Where reverence is lacking, injustice and violence prevail. Awe is essential for harmony among people as well as for harmony between human beings and the rest of creation.

Awe is a categorical imperative also because it is a prerequisite of wisdom. Whereas some people might tend to regard awe as an intellectual resignation, an end to wisdom, Heschel reminds us that according to the Psalmist (Ps 111:10) "*the awe of God is the beginning of wisdom*" and that in the Book of Job (28:28) "*the awe of God is wisdom.*"[20]

In fact, says Heschel, "the only way to wisdom is . . . through our relationship to God," which means that someone "who wishes to understand the world must seek to understand God."[21] What, possibly, can Heschel mean by this? He knows that there are many intelligent agnostics and atheists who understand a great deal about the world. So is he suggesting that to understand the *ultimate meaning* of the world, not just certain things about the world, we must seek to understand it in relation to God and, in doing so, seek some understanding of God?

Whatever he means, believers in God would do well to keep in mind Heschel's claim that people often know God "unknowingly" and fail to know God "when insisting upon knowing."[22] If this is true, then might it be that wherever there is an understanding for the *meaning* of things in this world—whether it is the understanding of an agnostic, an atheist, or a believer in God—there is some understanding of God, however tacit or explicit that understanding might be?

The understanding of God that may be born of awe is not a matter of *comprehending* the divine essence but of *apprehending* the divine presence and what it implies: "the ability to look at things from the point of view of God, sympathy with the divine pathos, the identification of the will with the will of God."[23] This, precisely, is what Heschel means by wisdom, and this "wisdom is fostered by awe."[24] And since "one needs wisdom of the spirit to know what it means to worship God,"[25] awe, like wonder, is both a prerequisite and an essential aspect of the worship of God.

Worship as an Expression of Gratitude and Love

Within our wonder and awe in response to the sublime mystery of existence, we realize that the world and we who are privileged to behold it and be a part of its miraculous unfolding are precious gifts for which we must be forever grateful. Worship is our expression of this gratitude.

Discerning the divine presence to which the world in its ineffable grandeur alludes, and recognizing the revelation of this presence conveyed through the Bible and biblical tradition, we are moved to worship the God who blesses us with this life-giving presence, this life-guiding revelation.

"No one is without a sense of awe, a need to adore, an urge to worship. The question only is what to adore, or more specifically, what object is worthy of our supreme worship."[26] According to Heschel and the Judaism he represents, many people and things merit our awe, even our praise; God alone, as the ultimate source of being and of our life's meaning, is worthy of our worship, our ultimate praise.

"Praise is the harvest of love," writes Heschel.[27] And as act of love for God, praise is always a personal, and in some sense even a private, response to God. It should be understood "as an enterprise of the individual self, as a personal engagement, as an intimate, confidential act."[28]

Nevertheless, praise or worship is never a merely solitary act. For instance, even when praying privately, "a Jew never worships as an isolated individual but as a part of *the Community of Israel*," says Heschel. "Yet it is within the heart of every individual that prayer takes place."[29] And not only does a Jew—or anyone else—pray as an individual in the context of a particular community, but also in league with all other human beings who do now or who ever have raised their hearts to God. "Every act of worship is an act of participating in an eternal service, in the service of all souls of all ages."[30]

Moreover, the "eternal service" of praise in which we partake extends beyond the realm of the human community. "We are not alone in our acts of praise. Wherever there is life, there is silent worship," declares Heschel.[31] "Our kinship with nature is a kinship of praise. All beings praise God. We live in a community of praise."[32]

It is our privilege and our vocation as human beings to articulate the "silent worship" of all things, to intone the score of eternal cosmic praise. "When we sing, we sing for all things," writes Heschel. "The universe is a score of eternal music, and we are the cry, we are the voice."[33]

But sometimes, like the worship given by other creatures, our worship is also silent, our cry of prayer without words. Heschel captures this in one of his early poems: "A soundless song weeps out of me — / longing mixed with happiness and thanks."[34] Such wordless praying occurs not only when our prayer is unconscious and merely implied, but even at times when we are fully attentive to God, hard at the work of worship. For words are not the only means of explicitly praising God. "In a sense, prayer begins where expression ends. The words that reach our lips are often but waves of an overflowing stream touching the shore. . . . The wave of a song carries the soul to heights which utterable meanings can never reach."[35]

"The sense for the power of words and the sense for the impotence of human expression," Heschel reminds us, "are equally characteristic of the religious consciousness."[36] Appropriately, then, Jewish worship consists of "words sanctified by ages of worship" as well as "the unutterable surplus of what we feel, the sentiments that we are unable to put into words."[37] So just as it is a distinctively human task "to utter, so to speak, what is in the heart of all things," it is equally human to "learn silence from the forests, from the stars—to go towards God."[38] Our worship may occur when "soul and sky are silent together" and when, in our words and songs, "the secret of cosmic prayer is disclosed."[39]

While the idea of cosmic prayer may sound like a fantasy to some people, for Heschel it is a truth discerned through participating in the endless song at the heart of creation. "The whole cosmos, every living being sings, the psalmists insist. Neither joy nor sorrow but song is the ground-plan of being. It is the quintessence of life. To praise is to call forth the promise and presence of the divine. We live for the sake of a song. We praise for the privilege of being. Worship is the climax of living. There is no knowledge without love, no truth without praise."[40]

But where there is love, there too is knowledge. And when love breaks into praise, there is an understanding of truth. Since "praise is the harvest of love," it is also the fruit of love's knowledge. It is not only the feeling of love that moves us to praise God but also the wisdom that love yields. "This is decisive: worship comes out of insight."[41]

And what is the insight of love out of which worship comes? Is it not precisely the realization that the meaning of existence is found in love, that we are indebted for existence graced with love, and that "in loving we intone God's unfinished song"?[42]

Worship as a Means of Sanctifying Time

While Heschel regards worship as a way of confirming our connection with the realm of nature, he also focuses on how it is concerned with the realm of time. "Judaism is a *religion of time* aiming at *the sanctification of time*," and Jewish ritual provides a means of sanctifying time. As Heschel explains: "Jewish ritual may be characterized as the art of significant forms in time, as *architecture of time*. Most of its observances—the Sabbath, the New Moon, the festivals, the Sabbatical and Jubilee year—depend on a certain hour of the day or season of the year. . . . The main themes of faith lie in the realm of time."[43]

The realm of time with which Jewish ritual is concerned includes in a special way the historical time of the Jewish people. "Judaism is a religion of history," and "genuine history is enshrined in our rituals."[44] Many Jewish rituals are ways of recalling and celebrating significant historic events, such as the exodus from Egypt and the revelation at Sinai.

It is important to stress the fact that Jewish rites *celebrate* these events, not simply commemorate them, for to celebrate them is, in a sense, to make them present, to feel their eternal relevance. Heschel claims that "there are events which never become past," that "days of the spirit never pass away."[45] Yet in order for such events and days to be kept alive they must be remembered, and ritual is one of the principal ways to remember and thus keep alive the past. "Jewish liturgy in text and song is a spiritual summary of our history,"[46] says Heschel, so participating in liturgy is a primary way of remembering Jewish history and, thus, the presence of God in that history.

"Words of prayer are repositories of the spirit," and to understand the spirit of Judaism "we must learn to face the grandeur of words" found in Jewish prayers.[47] "In Judaism study is a form of worship, but it may also be said that worship is in a sense a form of study; it includes meditation. It is not enough to rely on one's voice. It takes a constant effort to find a way to the grandeur of the words in the Prayer Book."[48]

Studying the words of the Jewish prayers, reciting them, chanting them, remembering what they represent, a person may be transported to the threshold of faith or strengthened in the life of faith. "It is more inspiring to let the heart echo the music of the ages than to play upon the broken flutes of our own hearts," writes Heschel. "There is always an opportunity to disclose the holy, but when we fail to seize it, there are definite moments in the liturgical order of the day, there are words in the liturgical order of our speech to remind us. These words are like mountain peaks pointing to the unfathomable. Ascending their trails we arrive at prayer."[49]

Prayer as Empathy and Expression

Implicit in this last quotation is a distinction between two types of prayer that Heschel elsewhere makes explicit: "prayer as *an act of expression* and prayer as *an act of empathy*."[50] In the first type a person addresses God in her or his own words, or in sighs beyond words. In the second type a person empathizes, or tries to empathize, with the words of prescribed prayers.

Heschel realizes that "prayer is an outburst of the heart, an act of spontaneity and self-expression."[51] He even claims that "spontaneity is the goal" of prayer.[52] But he also realizes that prayer may "begin by turning to the words of the liturgy" and that "continuity is the way" to attain the goal of prayer.[53] "It is the continuity of trying to pray, the unbroken loyalty of our duty to pray, that lends strength to our fragile worship."[54]

What better way to try to pray than to attempt to empathize with prayerful words?

Prayer of expression comes about when we feel the urge to pray. But we might not feel this urge as often as it would be good for us to pray. No such urge is needed for prayer of empathy to commence, just the realization that we have a "duty to pray," or just the suspicion that we may find prayer to be a meaningful act. "There need be no prayerful mood in us when we begin to pray. It is through our reading and feeling the words of the prayers, through the imaginative projection of our consciousness into the meaning of the words, and through empathy for the ideas with which the words are pregnant, that this type of prayer comes to pass."[55]

While Heschel makes a distinction between prayer as an act of expression and prayer as an act of empathy, he also speaks of them as related: "An act of empathy is involved in genuine expression, and profound empathy generates expression."[56] Ritual prayer, comprised of words that evoke the remembrance of God's revelation in history, may evoke heartfelt expression of gratitude to God, worship of God.

To worship God is an act of faith in God that nurtures faithfulness to God. But Heschel is suggesting that there is also a form of praying that may, in some sense, precede worship as an experience of faith. The prayer of empathy, the attempt to feel the meaning of ritual words, may be a prayer for the ability to worship, a prayer for the birth of faith. "The words are often the givers, and we the recipients. They inspire our minds and awaken our hearts."[57] After empathizing with the words of prayer, which is itself a form of prayer, we may arrive at the kind of prayer that is a form of faith.

And what was a prelude to faith may become an aspect of faith. We may ride the tide of ritual prayer with the hope of arriving at the shore of faith. And once upon the shore we may continue to plunge into ritual prayer in order to purify our faith. Even after the flowering of faith we might not always feel the urge to express our faith. Ritual prayer is an opportunity to recall the source of faith, to cultivate the soil of faith. Jewish ritual prayer thus fosters the genesis and the growth of Jewish faith in God.

Learning

The Jewish tradition is enshrined not only in liturgical texts of worship but also in other sacred texts, foremost among them the Bible and rabbinic literature. Jewish faith in God is therefore cultivated and expressed not only by way of ritual worship but also by way of religious study, primarily the study of biblical and rabbinic literature.

Study as a Form of Worship

While in some sense distinct from liturgical worship, the sacred study that precedes, nurtures, and expresses Jewish faith is not detached from the ritual prayer that leads to and reflects faith in God. To function as a pathway to faith or an expression of faith, study must be either rooted in or imbued with prayer. "The test of authentic theology is the degree to which it reflects and enhances the power of prayer, the way of worship," says Heschel. "Authentic theology is . . . scholarly, disciplined thinking grafted upon prayer."[58] As such, "study is *a form of worship*."[59]

Religious study that is simply a matter of curiosity or that is performed simply for the acquisition of knowledge is not study as worship. For it to be a sacred act, "study, learning must coincide with striving for intimate attachment to the Lord," says Heschel. "It must be raised to the level of prayer, become a kind of praying, not merely understanding."[60]

Although study without prayer does not necessarily nurture or express faith, students need not wait until they have the urge to pray before engaging in religious study. In fact, study may be a pathway to prayer, as prayer may in turn provoke more fruitful study. When study precedes prayer it may function much like prayer of empathy that precedes prayer of expression. And prayer of expression may be an impetus to engage not only in formal liturgical prayer but also in further study. Religious study, therefore, may serve as a pathway to faith and also be an expression of faith.

The Sacred Task of Teaching

Since study is so important to Jewish faith, so too is teaching, for genuine study is inspired by authentic teaching. Such teaching must first and foremost convey a deep appreciation for study: "Genuine reverence for the sanctity of study is bound to evoke in the pupils the awareness that study is not an ordeal but an act of edification; that the school is *a sanctuary*, not a factory."[61]

"Learning is holy, an indispensable form of purification as well as ennoblement," writes Heschel. "By learning I do not mean memorization, erudition; I mean the very act of study, of being involved in wisdom."[62] This is why "the unique attitude of the Jew is not the love of knowledge but the love of studying."[63] The teacher's vocation is to inspire the love of studying and thereby "to enable the pupil to participate and share in the spiritual experience of Jewish living," which is a matter of learning "what it means to live in the likeness of God."[64]

In Heschel's view, the teacher is called upon to represent and interpret humanity's most sacred possessions. The teacher of Judaism, in particular, is "the intermediary between the past and the present" as well as "the creator of the future of our people."[65] Such a teacher must not only possess knowledge but also be a vehicle of wisdom, and this wisdom must be conveyed not only in words but also in living: "What we need more than anything else is not *textbooks* but *textpeople*. It is the personality of the teacher which is the text that the pupils read; the text that they will never forget."[66] It is every teacher's duty to bear witness to the truth that every human being "is capable of genuine love and compassion, of discipline and universality of judgment, of moral and spiritual exaltation."[67]

For all of the esteem in which Heschel holds the teaching profession, he nonetheless claims that "education is a matter which rests primarily with the parent."[68] He is as earnest as ever, and perhaps most self-revealing, when speaking about the "supreme educational duty" of parents:

> The mainspring of tenderness and compassion lies in reverence. It is our supreme educational duty to enable the child to revere. The heart of the Ten Commandments is to be found in the words: *Revere thy father and thy mother.* Without profound reverence for father and mother, our ability to observe the other commandments is dangerously impaired. The problem we face, the problem I as a father face, is why my child should revere me. Unless my child will sense in my personal existence acts and attitudes that evoke reverence—the ability to delay satisfactions, to overcome prejudices, to sense the holy, to strive for the noble—why would she revere me? . . . Only a person who lives in a way which is compatible with the mystery of human existence is capable of evoking reverence in the child.[69]

From this it is clear that, for Heschel, education is first and foremost meant to be an "*education for reverence.*"[70] And since "reverence . . . is at the root of faith,"[71] Jewish education is about the cultivation of faith, both individual and communal faith in God.

For Heschel, the realization of personal uniqueness is an essential component of human existence, and Judaism is committed to fostering this realization. "No two human beings are alike. . . . Every human being has something to say, to think, or to do which is unprecedented."[72] Jewish education must communicate the spiritual substance of Judaism in such a way as to inspire unprecedented individual contributions that will enrich the Jewish community: "The endeavor to integrate the abiding teachings and aspirations of the past into our own thinking will enable us to be creative, to expand, not to imitate or to repeat."[73]

As a covenantal religion, Judaism is the antithesis of individualism. Yet, "it would be suicidal to reduce Judaism to communalism, collectivism, or nationalism."[74] Judaism is both the faith of a people and "the religion of the individual."[75] Therefore, religious education must help the individual to become a representative of the people and it must teach the people to accept and promote the uniqueness of each individual. True learning promotes individuality by stimulating "ingenuity and independence of mind, encouraging the students to create new out of old ideas."[76] At the same time "true learning is a way of relating oneself to something which is both *eternal* and *universal*" as it "counteracts *tribalism* and *self-centeredness.*"[77]

Because Judaism is a religion of the individual as well as of the people, and because individuality and community are essential characteristics of the human condition, Jewish education must foster both solitude and solidarity. There is no sense of individual identity, no sense of human dignity, without a sense of solitariness, without "the capacity to stand apart, to differ, to resist, and to defy."[78] And there is no sense of communal identity without actual solidarity. "We must all live in two spheres—in society and in privacy. To survive in society we must thrive in privacy."[79] Therefore, education must reach the inner life of individual students and help them to "know what to do in privacy," not only to "know how to act in public."[80]

"External performance is important, but it must be accompanied by the soul. The mind, the heart are not exempted from being engaged in the service of God."[81] Even an education for public life demands an education of the inner life. Ultimately, Jewish education is "character education [that] can only be carried out in depth, as *cultivation of total sensitivity,*" which Heschel explains as follows: "To educate means to cultivate the soul, not only the mind. You cultivate the soul by cultivating empathy and reverence for others, by calling attention to the grandeur, the mystery of all being, to the holy dimension of human existence by teaching how to relate the common to the spiritual. The soul is discovered in response, in acts of transcending the self, in the awareness of ends that surpass one's interests and needs."[82]

Education as a Life-long Process

For Heschel, such education is "a life-long process rather than a passing state," for "the attainment of wisdom is the work of a life time."[83]

He therefore stresses the dire need for adult education and even education for retirement. "It is wrong to define education as *preparation* for life," explains Heschel. "Learning *is* life, a supreme experience of living, a climax of existence. . . . The meaning of existence is found in the experience of education. Termination of education is the beginning of despair. Every person bears the responsibility for the legacy of the past as well as the burden of the future."[84]

Concerning the need of an education for retirement, Heschel is as insightful as ever: "May I suggest that . . . old age be regarded not as the age of stagnation but as *the age of opportunities for inner growth*? . . . The years of old age may enable us to attain the high values we failed to sense, the insights we missed, the wisdom we ignored. They are formative years, rich in possibilities to unlearn the follies of a lifetime, to see through inbred self deceptions, to deepen understanding and compassion, to widen the horizon of honesty, to refine the sense of fairness."[85]

Like nearly all of his insights, Heschel's ideas about education, including how it should be an ongoing adventure of the spirit for all members of society, are rooted in his own Jewish learning and experience. Reminiscing about the style of Jewish life that he knew in Poland before the Holocaust, Heschel writes:

> In almost every Jewish home in Eastern Europe, even in the humblest and the poorest, stood a bookcase full of volumes, proud and stately folio tomes together with shy, small-sized books. Books were neither an asylum for the frustrated nor a means for occasional edification. They were furnaces of living strength, timeproof receptacles for the eternally valid coins of the spirit. . . . To some people, it was impossible to pray without having been refreshed first by spending some time in the sublime atmosphere of Torah. Others, after the morning prayer, would spend an hour with their books before starting to work. . . .
>
> Poor Jews, whose children knew only the taste of "potatoes on Sunday, potatoes on Monday, potatoes on Tuesday," sat there like intellectual magnates. They possessed whole treasures of thought, a wealth of information, of ideas and sayings of many ages. . . . The stomachs were empty, the homes barren, but the minds were crammed with the riches of Torah.[86]

"The riches of Torah" are known to those who study it with care. And the treasures of a tradition based on the Torah are remembered to a great extent by devoted study. While Heschel realizes, with the Baal Shem Tov, that a person could be devoted to the study of the Torah and still remain distant from God, he also recalls another of the Baal Shem's teachings: "Torah study is a way of coming upon the presence of God."[87]

The outcome of Torah study depends on the motive for and the approach to that study. If it is pursued for the sake of self-aggrandizement, the student of the Torah might remain distant from God. If pursued for the sake of discovering truth and living by it, Torah study may help the student begin to sense the presence of God or to deepen it.

Since "the way that always leads to God is Truth,"[88] the search for truth is, knowingly or not, a search for God. The search for truth prepares us to perceive the revelation of truth. And since "Truth is always with God,"[89] the revelation of truth is a revelation from God. Faith in God is a response to the truth recognized as divine. Genuine study, as a quest for truth, may prepare the way for such a response and thereby foster faith in God.

Action

Worship and learning are, to be sure, forms of action. So when Heschel distinguishes "worship, learning, and action" as the main aspects of Jewish religious life, clearly he is using the term "action" in this context to refer to deeds other than explicit acts of worship and learning. Perhaps primary among the other deeds that Heschel has in mind are deeds of charity, for in another context he reminds us that "according to an ancient Hebrew saying, the world rests upon three pillars: upon *learning*, upon *worship*, and upon *charity*."[90] But throughout his writings Heschel focuses on many different types of action, not only deeds of charity, along with learning and worship, that he considers to be divine expectations—for example, acts of healing, justice, mercy, compassion, love, and peacemaking.

"The Primary Way of Serving God"

Within the Jewish tradition, Heschel insists, worshiping God and studying Torah must not be dissonant with the rest of living. "Unless living is a form of worship, our worship has no life," he writes, and "acts of loving-kindness and study of Torah must go together."[91] In fact, Heschel suggests that deeds of loving-kindness are even more important than Torah study and explicit acts of worship. "Study should be a means, not an end in itself," he writes after quoting from the Talmud: "Great is the study of Torah because it leads to action."[92] And while worship of God is an end in itself, Heschel claims that "worship without compassion is worse than self-deception; it is an abomination."[93]

It is unthinkable that Heschel would ever say the reverse, that deeds of compassion by those who abstain from worship are an abomination. Although he would want to inspire worship in the lives of those who, for whatever reasons, do not explicitly acknowledge God, he would not ever think that good deeds divorced from explicit acts of worship were anything but good. But Heschel does share what he regards as the God-inspired view of prophetic Judaism, "that the worth of worship, far from being absolute, is contingent upon moral living, and that when immorality prevails, worship is detestable."[94] Heschel trusts that God welcomes our worship, and he knows that God alone is worthy of worship, but, with the prophets of Israel, he believes that "the primary way of serving God is through love, justice, and righteousness."[95]

No Dichotomy between Faith and Works

Just as worship of God and Torah study express Jewish faith, so does ethical action. "God reaches us as a claim," writes Heschel. "Religious responsibility is responsiveness to the claim. . . . The task of the Jew is a life in which the word [the claim] becomes deed."[96] Ethical deeds may be deliberate responses to the revelation of God's concern and challenge and thus be expressions of faith.

"The dichotomy of faith and works which presented such an important problem in Christian theology was never a problem in Judaism," writes Heschel. "To us, the basic problem is neither what is the right action nor what is the right intention. The basic problem is: what is right living? And life is indivisible. The inner sphere is never isolated from outward activities."[97]

To be sure, Heschel is a champion of "the inner sphere," and it would be difficult to imagine anyone writing more compellingly than he about the inner life, about the importance of *kavanah*, of right intention and soulful attentiveness to God. We each must cultivate an inner life, performing internal deeds, acts of mind, heart, and soul. Faith, to a large extent, is comprised of such internal acts, but not solely. Faith is also comprised of external deeds done with spirit, with kavanah. "Faith is not a silent treasure to be kept in the seclusion of the soul, but a mint in which to strike the coin of common deeds."[98] Moreover, Jewish faith is not just a matter of single deeds performed here and there, now and then, but of a pattern of deeds that constitutes an order of living. "It is right that the good actions should become a habit, that the preference of justice should become our second nature; even though it is not native to the self."[99]

As much as Heschel stresses the importance of kavanah, he never suggests that we should wait for purity of motivation before enacting good deeds. Nor does he suggest that the good in those deeds is vitiated for want of pure intention. "An action has intrinsic meaning; its value to the world is independent of what it means to the person performing it. The act of giving food to a helpless child is meaningful regardless of whether or not the moral intention is present. God asks for the heart, and we must spell our answer in terms of deeds."[100]

"God asks for the heart, but the heart is oppressed with uncertainty in its own twilight," writes Heschel. "God asks for faith, and the heart is not sure of its own faith. It is good that there is a dawn of decision for the night of the heart; deeds to objectify faith, definite forms to verify belief."[101] Yes, faith is an act of the heart, but "the heart is revealed in the deeds."[102]

Of course, good deeds do not always reveal faith in God. Often they are enacted in the absence of such faith. And, obviously, good deeds performed by agnostics and atheists may be every bit as good as those performed by believers in God. But just as prayer and Torah study may water the roots of faith before they become expressions of its flowering, so it may be with other actions. "By living as Jews we may attain our faith as Jews," writes Heschel. "We do not have faith because of deeds; we may attain faith through sacred deeds."[103] One reason for this is that in doing good deeds we may come to suspect that we are responding to a transcendent challenge—an obligation that transcends, and at times counters, our inclinations—to enact the good. Another reason we may attain faith through good deeds is because we may come to sense that, however humanly free they may be, these deeds are empowered by more than human power.

Recognizing that "concern for others often demands the price of self-denial," Heschel suggests that this concern is not adequately explained as "self-extension" but as an "ascension" beyond the self, which is made possible by "the sense of the ineffable that leads us beyond the horizon of personal interests, helping us to realize the absurdity of regarding the ego as an end."[104] We may attain faith through good deeds because, enacting them, we may sense that these deeds, though freely performed, have a source that transcends and empowers human initiative. In Heschel's words, we may come "to believe in the *immanence of God in deeds*."[105]

Just as the performance of good deeds may lead to faith in God, so it may, for those who have this faith, lead to kavanah. "Deeds not only follow intention; they also engender kavanah," writes Heschel. "There is no static polarity of kavanah and deed, of devotion and action. The deed may bring out what is dormant in the mind. . . . Kavanah comes into being with the deed. Actions teach."[106]

And the flow of good actions remains necessary even with the ebbing of kavanah. "While love is hibernating, our loyal deeds speak."[107] And the best chance of rekindling the fire of love is to continue enacting deeds that bespeak love even when its fire is not felt. "How else can one learn the joy of loving-kindness, if not by enacting it?"[108] Yes, "religion is born of fire, of a flame, in which the dross of the mind and soul is melted away,"[109] but loyalty to religious conviction born of fire is every bit as important to the religious life as the fire that sparked the conviction. There is nothing inauthentic about acting out of loyalty to conviction when passion burns low or appears dormant. And fire in the soul is best rekindled by loyal deeds. "The soul grows by noble deeds. The soul is illumined by sacred acts."[110]

Delighting in Good Deeds

Although acts of goodness at times involve sacrifice and even self-denial, they also may be means of joy and pleasure for those performing them. "Perhaps this is one of the goals of Jewish education: to learn how to sense the ineffable delight of good deeds," writes Heschel. "The love and delight with which we do the good and the holy are the test of our spirit."[111]

While elsewhere he speaks of "the pleasure of good deeds,"[112] in the context from which this last statement is taken, Heschel makes a distinction between joy and pleasure, quoting W. R. Boyce Gibson on the subject: "I am pleased with an object when it gratifies some interest of mind or some instinctive impulse. It gives me pleasure if it fulfills my need. . . . But joy is not self-centered like pleasure. No doubt there is pleasure in it, for all our emotions are toned by pleasure or pain, but such pleasure is but the pleasure of the joy. . . . The joy itself attaches not to the subject but to the object, and to have joy in an object is to value it for its own sake."[113]

In light of this, it might be thought that when Heschel speaks of "the pleasure of good deeds" he is using the word "pleasure" as a synonym for "joy." But that need not be the case since, according to him, Judaism "rejects the idea that the good should be done in self-detachment, that the satisfaction felt in doing the good would taint the purity of the act."[114]

Throughout his writings Heschel insists that we should act not only, nor even primarily, to satisfy ourselves, our own needs, but to serve worthy ends that are in need of us. Nevertheless, he also thinks that we should not worry about deriving satisfaction from serving those ends. To the contrary, he says that "Jewish religious education consists in converting ends into personal needs" because "if those ends are not assimilated as needs but remain mere duties, uncongenial to the heart, incumbent but not enjoyed, then there is a state of tension between the self and the task."[115] And, according to Heschel, "the right relationship of the self to the good [the task] is not that of tension but that of inner agreement and accord."[116] When such accord takes place, both joy and pleasure may be felt in the fulfillment of duties, in serving ends that go beyond the self. "Judaism demands the full participation of the person in the service of the Lord; the heart rather than boycotting the acts of the will ought to respond in joy and undivided delight."[117]

The Task of Redemption

But while experiencing joy in the doing of good deeds is important, the granting of joy, bringing it to others, is even more important. Seeking personal joy as the primary goal of action would be like making personal salvation the ultimate goal of living, and Heschel reminds us that "what is urgent for the Jew is not the acceptance of salvation but the preparing of redemption, the preparing *for* redemption."[118] In this, each person has a role, and every deed counts. "The world is torn by conflicts, by folly, by hatred," writes Heschel. "Our task is to cleanse, to illumine, to repair. Every deed is either a clash or an aid in the effort of redemption."[119]

Heschel does not blame God for the world's evils. He believes they result from defiance of God's will, from rejection of God's love. In his view, God tries to prevent evil by accosting the consciences of those who do it and of those who can stop it. But when human beings ignore or reject divine commands, then what God wants is not achieved. And until God's desires are fulfilled the world will not be fully redeemed. For the world's redemption to be advanced, God needs the cooperation of human beings. In fact, in typically striking fashion, Heschel claims that "God is waiting for us to redeem the world."[120]

To be sure, Heschel affirms the traditional Jewish belief that God is not only the Creator but also, as the ultimate source of redemption, the Redeemer. Nevertheless, he asserts, "the keys that can unlock the chains fettering the Redeemer" are held by each of us.[121] Perhaps God will raise up an individual messiah to usher in the messianic age of universal peace. This has been a hope of Jews throughout the ages. But Heschel reminds us that within the Jewish tradition, redemption is thought of not "solely as an act that will come about all at once and without preparation" but as "an ongoing, continuous process in which all have a role to play, either retarding or enhancing the process."[122] We must enhance the process; we must prepare the world for the messianic arrival, which we can do because "the Messiah is in us."[123]

If we succeed, however humbly, in advancing the process of redemption, it will be "by the grace of God."[124] But just as we need God's grace to help redeem the world, so God needs our responsiveness to divine grace. But why? Is God not all-powerful? Heschel's answer: God's need for us is "a self-imposed concern," a concern to make us partners in the divine enterprise of creating and redeeming.[125] And, as we saw in the previous chapter, Heschel regards the idea of divine omnipotence as a non-Jewish idea.

If we stop thinking of omnipotence as an attribute of the divine, we will be free to appreciate as never before that the true mark of divinity—what makes God divine and thus worthy of our worship—is not absolute power and control but infinite compassion, unending love.

Such an understanding of God, and of God's need for our help in redeeming the world, is bound to have a profound effect on our way of responding to God. It may move us to have "compassion for God," which Heschel regards as an expression of faith in God.[126] And, what is more important, we may become convinced that "God needs not only sympathy and comfort but partners" in the task of redemption, and that the surest way for us to live up to our partnership with God is to enact "deeds in which God is at home in the world."[127]

CHAPTER FOUR

GOD AND RELIGIOUS DIVERSITY

Unwavering in his commitment to one particular religion, Heschel nonetheless claims that "diversity of religions is the will of God,"[1] a claim that is utterly consistent with his beliefs about the oneness of God and the diversity of human responses to God, about divine revelation and redemption, and about the relationship between faith in God and creedal statements about God. This chapter focuses on how each of these beliefs fosters Heschel's conviction about God and religious diversity.

The Oneness of God and the Diversity of Responses to God

Heschel's conviction that religious diversity is the will of God is rooted primarily in his understanding of God, particularly as this understanding is based on the foundational biblical claim that God is One, and on his appreciation for how human beings in various religious traditions respond to God.

God Is One

"Hear, O Israel, the Lord is our God, the Lord is One" (Deut 6:4, Heschel's translation). Among the several complementary interpretations that Heschel offers for this hallowed biblical verse, referred to as the *Sh'ma* after its first Hebrew word, he suggests as a principal meaning that "there is one being who is both Creator and Redeemer."[2] It is precisely because Heschel is convinced that the God revealed to and worshiped by the Jewish people is the one and only Creator and Redeemer of the whole world that he is able to perceive the presence of God in traditions other than his own. "Does not the all-inclusiveness of God contradict the exclusiveness of any particular religion?" asks Heschel. "Is it not blasphemous to say: I alone have all the truth and grace, and all those who differ live in darkness and are abandoned by the grace of God?"[3]

Reflecting on the *Sh'ma*, Heschel says that "unity of God is power for unity of God with all things."[4] And responding to the question, "What do we mean by the word 'God'?" Heschel states: "We mean that there is a divine concern embracing all of us."[5] It would be the height of arrogance to claim that one religion has a franchise on divine concern, and, in Heschel's words, "God is everywhere save in arrogance."[6] Ironically, then, to insist on possessing an exclusive way to God is, at least on this issue, to go astray from God.

"Religion is a means, not the end," writes Heschel. "It becomes idolatrous when regarded as an end in itself."[7] To assume that there is only one valid way of responding to God is—precisely by absolutizing that way—to equate a religious means with the divine end. And about this Heschel is emphatic: "To equate religion and God is idolatry."[8]

Genuine monotheistic faith demands an attitude of openness to the validity of various religions precisely because it is opposed to absolutizing—that is, deifying—anything other than God, including a cherished tradition that fosters faith in God. "We must not regard any human institution or object as being an end in itself," writes Heschel. "A temple that comes to mean more than a reminder of the living God is an abomination."[9]

But Heschel goes ever further, condemning as idolatrous not only our living as if our religion or anything about it is an end in itself but even our considering as ultimate a specific event or act of God's revelation that may be at the foundation of our religion: "We must not idolize the moment or the event [of revelation]. The will of God is eternal, transcending all moments, all events, including acts of revelation."[10] This, indeed, is radical monotheism: God transcends even God's revelation. God, and not any particular manifestation of God, is the ultimate reality.

So, contrary to what many people seem to assume, true monotheistic faith means that we must not make our faith the object of our faith. "There is great merit in having no absolute faith in our faith," writes Heschel. "Human faith is never final, never an arrival, but rather an endless pilgrimage, a being on the way. We have no answers to all problems. Even some of our most sacred answers are both emphatic and qualified."[11] Therefore, Heschel asserts emphatically: "To rely on our faith would be idol-worship. We have only the right to rely on God."[12]

The God of biblical faith is not simply the God of biblical traditions—let alone just the God of one biblical tradition. Therefore, those who stand within a biblical tradition should admit that God communes with human beings in and through various traditions, biblical and otherwise. "Respect for each other's commitment, respect for each other's faith, is more than a political and social imperative," writes Heschel. "It is born of the insight that God is greater than religion."[13] And this insight that he champions is rooted in his understanding of the *Sh'ma*: the one God, as both Creator and Redeemer of all people, is available to them all.

Clearly, Heschel has a God-centered, rather than a Torah-centered or Judaism-centered, view of the "universe of faiths." While remaining steadfast in his commitment to the way of Torah, and while even believing that Torah is irreplaceable in the world, Heschel claims that "the Torah is not an end in itself" because "God is greater than the Torah."[14] Thus, he says, "Jews do not maintain that the way of Torah is the only way of serving God."[15] While believing that it has "no substitutes," Heschel nonetheless acknowledges that "Judaism has allies,"[16] which is to say that, like Judaism, but apart from its way of Torah, there are other religions providing ways of serving God.

Nevertheless, although Heschel perceives diversity of religions as the will of God, he rejects "a vision of ultimate pluralism"—that is to say, a view of ultimate reality or divinity as plural—in favor of "the vision of the One," the view that "the spirit of unity hovers over the face of all plurality."[17] According to this latter vision, the One, the divine spirit of unity, does not absorb or erase the world's plurality. No, on the contrary, the One creates a world teeming with plurality, diversity. But this world is a *universe* with the necessary conditions for the possibility of *unity among diverse beings*. Monotheism, in Heschel's rendering of it, as opposed to polytheism, ignites an appreciation for the unity of all human beings— "There is no insight more disclosing: *God is One, and humanity is one*"— and, beyond that, an appreciation for "*the togetherness of all beings in holy otherness*."[18]

So while "polytheism seems to be more compatible with emotional moods and imagination," Heschel champions monotheism for providing "the idea of unity . . . upon which the ultimate justification of philosophical, ethical and religious universalism depends."[19] Amid all the discord tearing this world apart, our vision of the one God—indeed our experience of the presence of this God—may inspire us to accept and to discharge "the power to aid in bringing about ultimate unification."[20]

But Heschel's commitment to monotheism over against polytheism is based not only on this goal of ultimate unification but also on the conviction that monotheism is a more credible interpretation of reality. "Nothing we count, divide, or surpass—a fraction or plurality—can be taken as the ultimate," writes Heschel. "You cannot ask in regard to the divine: Which one? There is only one synonym for God: One."[21]

But Heschel seems to overstate his case for monotheism vis-à-vis polytheism when he claims that "plurality is incompatible with the sense of the ineffable" and that "to the sense of the ineffable the oneness of God is self-evident."[22] In fact, these claims are inconsistent with what Heschel writes elsewhere. In contrast to the first of these claims, Heschel suggests throughout his writings that life is filled with many ineffable mysteries. In contrast to the second of these claims, Heschel elsewhere asserts precisely the opposite: although it may lead to an awareness of God, "the sense of the ineffable does not give us an awareness of God."[23]

So rather than saying that the oneness of God is self-evident to the sense of the ineffable, perhaps Heschel should say that God's oneness is self-evident to *the sense of the ultimate*. Plurality is not incompatible with the sense of the ineffable; to the sense of the ineffable there are many ineffable realities. It is because of a sense of the ultimate that "you cannot ask in regard to the divine: Which one?"

"We ask about God," writes Heschel. "But what is the minimum of meaning that the word God holds for us? It is first the idea of *ultimacy*. . . . It means further One, unique, eternal."[24] Yes, it is to the sense of ultimacy that the oneness of God is self-evident, not to the sense of the ineffable, which many polytheists surely have in common with many monotheists.

What Heschel usually suggests about the relationship between the sense of the ineffable and the sense of God's presence is that the former may predispose us to the latter. The sense of the ineffable awakens the realization that reality is neither grounded in our own minds nor simply the result of something that human minds can grasp and account for scientifically. Realizing that reality is beyond our comprehension, we may begin to realize that life and time are not our own property. The awareness of the ineffable, that reality exceeds what we can comprehend and describe, prepares us to perceive the revelation of the Ineffable One who is even further beyond our comprehension than the ineffable realm of which we are a part.

But, we may ask, do we really have a sense, an awareness, of the oneness of ultimate reality—as opposed to a sense of the ultimate as plural—or is it just that we have a tradition that gives a monotheistic interpretation to our experiences of the ineffable? Recall that in chapter 1, when exploring Heschel's understanding of religious experience as involving a sense of transcendent concern and transcendent challenge, we asked a similar question—whether or not manifold experiences of transcendent concern and challenge might testify to a multiplicity of concerned and challenging deities rather than to one God. We then offered this answer as reflecting Heschel's perspective: Since the manifold experiences of the transcendent concern and transcendent challenge are all experiences of a unifying concern, of a challenge "to keep aflame our awareness of living in the great fellowship of all beings,"[25] for this reason the manifold experiences must be testifying to the presence of one creative source of unity, one unifying force or power, one God. Although experienced in myriad ways, the transcendent concern and challenge that drives us toward oneness must be supremely one.

Admittedly, perhaps many of us would not interpret these experiences as testifying to one source of unity, one God, were we not a part of a monotheistic tradition, but in accord with this tradition we are able to say whether or not the monotheistic interpretation fits our experiences. Experience usually precedes interpretation of it, at least an adequate interpretation. Often there are ingredients of an experience that we are not conscious of at the time of the experience but that come to light at a later time. We may, for example, experience love without recognizing it at the time. Later, sometimes too late, we may realize that we were being loved without appreciating it for what it was. Later we may respond to an initiative that almost went unnoticed.

Likewise, might God's presence not have been the source and substance of our experience without our having been able to recognize it? Might we not later come to recognize that God was there all along? Often we need guidance to interpret our experiences, especially our deep experiences. The monotheistic tradition based on the *Sh'ma*, on the assertion of the oneness of God, offers us guidance in interpreting our religious experiences. This tradition enables us to distinguish between the sense of the ineffable and the sense of the ultimate, to recognize that while abiding in the realm of the ineffable we experience the presence and the call of the Ineffable One.

Should we really be surprised that the presence of God is not discernable in ways that other presences are? Recall another claim made in chapter 1, that because God's being "transcends mysteriously all conceivable being,"[26] God's presence transcends all other types of presence. It is, so to speak, a disguised presence. But however disguised, because however transcendent of other presences, Heschel reminds us that "the certainty of being exposed to a presence not of this world is a fact of human existence."[27] Some people may sense this presence at distant intervals in their lives, while others may have an abiding sense of divine presence. Whatever the case may be, when human beings sense the presence of the divine they may also realize, through the guidance of a monotheistic tradition, that this presence transcends the ineffable realm through which it is disclosed, and that it is not simply one among a variety of supernatural presences, as might be assumed in a polytheistic tradition, but that it is an incomparable presence. Thus, says Heschel, "there is no equivalent of the divine."[28]

Because there is no equivalent of the divine, Heschel's commitment to monotheism is in opposition not only to polytheism but also to worldviews that deem as divine the world we know or any other conceivable world. When interpreting the *Sh'ma*—"Hear, O Israel, the Lord is our God, the Lord is One"—Heschel points out that, according to Jewish tradition, it means not simply that there is only one true God, but also that God possesses inner unity, which, in turn, is the necessary precondition for whatever unity is achieved in this world.

Pantheism is one way of explaining unity in the world. In the strictest sense of the term, pantheism is the belief that the world is divine (literally, "all is God"). This can be understood to mean that there is no more to God than the world, or it can mean that the world is an emanation (in contrast to a creation) of God. In this emanationist version of pantheism, which is more appropriately referred to as pan*en*theism, the world is divine without being all there is to the divine.[29]

The pantheistic and panentheistic claim that "all is God" is tantamount to saying that "all is One." But the "One" of this claim has parts; it can be divided—and indeed it is: "The world lies in strife, in discord, in divergence."[30] Therefore, pantheism and panentheism, regardless of intention, promote "a vision of ultimate pluralism" every bit as much as does polytheism. And because the world is full of both good and evil, the ultimate pluralism—that is, the plurally composed ultimate—of pantheism and panentheism contains not only good but also evil. And if the world is divine (even if, according to the panentheistic vision, the world is not all there is to the divine), then God is not entirely good. But if this is so, then what would make God worthy of our worship, which is to ask, what would make God really and truly God? And if evil is part of divinity, what motivation and hope could we have of ever overcoming evil with good?

In Heschel's view, the plurally composed ultimate of pantheism and panentheism is not truly ultimate—not truly God—because it can be and is divided and because it contains evil. Only monotheism's indivisible

God, precisely as indivisible—"not partly here and partly there," but "all here and all there"[31]—and thus mysteriously present to all creatures, is truly ultimate. Only monotheism's all-good God, precisely as infinitely good—"not beyond good and evil"[32]—and thus the source of the goodness with which we may combat evil, is worthy of our worship.

And not only is God devoid of evil; "God is not indifferent to evil!" exclaims Heschel.[33] This realization—in contrast to the pantheistic and panentheistic views of the world (with all the evils it includes) as divine—can provide us with the motivation and the hope that we need to try to overcome evil with good. "We are never alone in our struggle with evil," writes Heschel. "In the light of the Bible, the good is more than a value; it is a *divine concern*, a way of God. . . . We do not wage war with evil in the name of an abstract concept of duty. We do the good not because it is a value or because of expediency, but because we owe it to God."[34]

Yes, we owe it to God because the gift and the challenge to do the good come from God. "God" is the name we give to the infinitely good and challenging transcendent source of the good with which we do good. Whatever includes evil—no matter that it also includes good—does not deserve to be considered ultimate, to be called God, to be worshiped. Besides, believing that the world is divine can lead to the fatalistic acceptance of evil as inevitable; believing that "beyond all evil is the compassion of God" may convince us that the "power of love" will enable us "to overcome the powers of evil."[35]

Although Heschel clearly proclaims the biblical belief that "the world is not the *all*,"[36] due to his emphasis on God's all-pervasive presence in the world and on how the world dwells within the sphere of God, some of his readers describe his religious perspective as panentheistic, which they recognize as distinct from a pantheistic perspective.[37] But since the term "panentheistic" is usually used to suggest that everything exists in God as part of God, is it not misleading to use this term to describe Heschel's religious outlook?

To be sure, some of Heschel's statements—such as his reference to God as "*being in and beyond all beings*"[38]—read out of context may lend themselves to a panentheistic interpretation. But he emphatically asserts that "God is not all in all," that "the world is not of the essence of God," that "nature is not a part of God."[39] Clearly, for Heschel, while God's being is within all beings, it is not in them as a part of them, and all beings are not parts of God's being.

In Heschel's monotheistic worldview, God does not include the world but embraces it, which means that "all existence is coexistence with

God."[40] Therefore, "we are not told to decide between 'Either-Or,' either God or the world," but "to accept Either and Or, God and the world."[41] In Heschel's view, "the adoration of nature is as absurd as the alienation from nature is unnecessary."[42] So with full appreciation of the sublime mystery of nature, Heschel affirms the reality of God as distinct from, though intimately present to, the world that God creates and loves.

There are pantheists and panentheists who suggest that monotheism, as opposed to the idea of a divine universe, leads to human separation from nature and even to human disregard and mistreatment of the things of this world. But the demand of authentic monotheistic faith, like that espoused by Heschel, is precisely the opposite—it is, as we have noted, the demand to acknowledge "the sacred relevance of all being" and "to keep aflame our awareness of living in the great fellowship of all beings."[43]

So while Heschel's monotheism is in opposition to polytheism, pantheism, and panentheism, it nonetheless inspires him to recognize God's presence within communities that are not monotheistic. Basic to Heschel's Jewish faith is the conviction that God loves all people and that God has given peoples of many faiths an awareness of divine love. "God is to be found in many hearts all over the world," says Heschel, "not limited to one nation or to one people, to one religion."[44] Religions may be considered valid or true to the extent that they foster this awareness of divine love—as also love for God. And even those non-monotheistic religions that do not explicitly espouse the love of God and love for God may be considered valid to the extent that they foster love for human beings, which, for Heschel, "is a way of worshiping God, a way of loving God."[45] All religions that cultivate such love are, from his perspective, valid and vital ways of serving God.

Diverse Human Responses to God

If, as Heschel asserts, "God is to be found in many hearts all over the world," in his view it is not only because of who God is and how God relates to diverse peoples but also because these diverse peoples have a diversity of fruitful responses to God. And, for him, it is obvious that people in various religious traditions usually respond to God not in spite of their traditions but in the context of them and because of them.

Heschel is convinced that concrete history is the arena of human experiences of God, and he insists that God transcends all historical manifestations of divine presence. Thus he would have no affinity for a concept of Judaism analogous to Karl Rahner's "anonymous Christianity" to explain the responsiveness to God apart from his own tradition. Rahner (1904–84), perhaps the most influential Catholic theologian of the twentieth century, rejects the exclusivist claim that only those who are explicitly Christian are in communion with God, but he attempts to give some sense to the ancient Christian teaching that there is "no salvation outside the church" by suggesting that some people may have implicit or "anonymous" membership in the church. Since Rahner believes that God's grace is always and everywhere mediated by Christ as the sole savior of the world, and because he believes that the church is the vehicle of that grace, he thinks that people who are not explicitly Christian but who nonetheless experience divine grace have an implied experience of Christ and an anonymous membership in the church. They can, therefore, be considered "anonymous Christians."[46]

While Heschel also believes that people who are not explicitly monotheists may nonetheless experience and respond to God implicitly, that they may know God "unknowingly," he does not suggest that this makes them implied or anonymous Jews. He simply does not presume that people either have to be Jewish or somehow related to Judaism, even if only implicitly, in order to live in accord with God.

Heschel and Rahner, of course, share the belief that all grace comes ultimately from one infinite source and center of existence, one God. But, unlike Rahner, Heschel does not believe that all grace flows through one finite channel, one religion. Perhaps because he believes that there are people who are not explicit monotheists who nonetheless experience and respond to divine grace, Heschel would not be opposed to the term "anonymous monotheists" to describe them. But because Heschel does not regard his Judaism in the same way that Rahner regards his Christianity—as, in Rahner's words, "the absolute religion, intended for all men, which cannot recognize any other religion beside itself as of equal right"[47]—Heschel would not accept the idea of an "anonymous Judaism."[48]

Precisely because God is God, monotheists must see the good actions of all people, including non-monotheists, as bearing witness to God. And precisely because religion is not God, monotheists must reject the idea that all good people be defined in terms of a given religion.

There is a world of difference between the idea of an implicit or anonymous monotheist and the idea of an anonymous Christian or Jew because God, not any given religion, is the source and center of all being and meaning. It is one thing to suggest, as Heschel does, that all grace comes from the infinite source and center of existence; it is quite another thing to suggest, as Rahner does, that all grace comes through something that is finite, the church.

Heschel's attitude reflects the universalist spirit of Judaism's early sages who recognized righteousness and sanctity among Gentiles. Harold Kasimow, a leading interpreter of Heschel's approach to religious diversity, reminds us that "the Jewish tradition has never denied that saints are produced outside Judaism," but, he also notes, more than most Jewish theologians Heschel emphasizes this idea, which "holds great promise for the future of interreligious dialogue and for the enrichment of the Jewish tradition."[49]

Already in 1955, a decade before declaring his belief that "diversity of religions is the will of God," Heschel acknowledged that it has been "vitally important . . . for Judaism to reach out into non-Jewish cultures in order to absorb elements which it may use for the enrichment of its life and thought."[50] And this theme of enrichment through contact with people apart from one's own religious community is central to Heschel's 1965 address on religious diversity: "The purpose of religious communication among human beings of different commitments is mutual enrichment and enhancement of respect and appreciation."[51]

Of course, such an approach to interreligious relations takes humility, and Heschel is to the point on this topic: "Religion is often inherently guilty of the sin of pride and presumption. To paraphrase the prophet's words, the exultant religion dwelt secure and said in her heart: 'I am, there is no one besides me.' Humility and contrition seem to be absent where most required—in theology. But humility is the beginning and end of religious thinking, the secret test of faith. There is no truth without humility, no certainty without contrition."[52]

As important as humility is, Heschel would probably say that it is simple honesty that compels him to acknowledge that "holiness is not the monopoly of any particular religion or tradition" and, therefore, "conversion to Judaism is no prerequisite for sanctity."[53] Needless to say, the fact that Heschel sees holiness or sanctity in various religious traditions and thus considers diversity of religions as the will of God does not mean that he regards all religions as equal, whatever that could mean. But since those who affirm the validity of various religions are often thought to be (or accused of) suggesting the equality of religions, it may be worth noting that Heschel never makes this claim. "None of us pretends to be God's accountant,"[54] says Heschel (though it might have been more realistic for him to say that none of us should pretend to be God's accountant!), and thus he never pretends to be able to make such a judgment.

Likewise, the fact that Heschel sees holiness or sanctity in different religions does not mean that he regards all—or even most—of what goes by the name of religion as promoting holiness or sanctity and thus reflective of God's will. To the contrary, Heschel frequently points out that much of what is called "religion" undermines human dignity, promotes violence, and is an affront to God. Still, he insists that "religion's task is to cultivate disgust for violence and lies, sensitivity to other people's suffering, and love of peace."[55] When religions in their many and diverse ways fulfill this common task they prove themselves to be valid and vital pathways to God.

Divine Revelation and Redemption

Implicit in the above, and also directly connected to his understanding of religious diversity as the will of God, are Heschel's views about divine revelation and redemption. While most of his writing about revelation focuses on God's revelation to the Jewish people, the topic we explored in chapter 2, Heschel also suggests that Jews are not the only recipients of divine revelation. And while his writing about redemption, which we touched upon at the end of chapter 3, frequently deals with the Jewish obligation to assist God in the task of redemption, just as frequently Heschel indicates that this task is incumbent upon all people.

Revelation in a Multiplicity of Languages

Although Jewish theologians generally have been open to the idea of there being diverse pathways to God, usually they have held that their own religion was the only one to be formed and sustained in response to divine revelation. At the core of Judaism is faith in one God, Creator and Redeemer of the world, whose love and will have been revealed to the Jewish people, a covenanted people fashioned by God to be a vehicle of divine revelation to the rest of the world. As a "chosen people," the Jews have been charged with the task of giving witness to God by way of Torah.

But just as the biblical and rabbinic authors reminded the people that their being a chosen people did not imply either their superiority in relation to other peoples or an exclusive relationship with God, Heschel points out that it does not imply that the Jewish people are the only vehicle of God's revelation. He indicates this in a number of ways. At the most basic level, Heschel insists that God is, or may be, revealed through each and every human being: "The human is the disclosure of the divine. . . . To meet a human being is an opportunity to sense the image of God, *the presence* of God."[56] Although the Jewish people are chosen for a special type of witness, every human being, created in the image of God, is meant to be "*a witness for God*."[57]

While the claim that every person, created in the image of God, may somehow reveal the presence of God and be a witness for God is a traditional Jewish teaching, Heschel goes beyond this in suggesting that Judaism is not the only religion of divine revelation. Speaking specifically about different religious traditions, Heschel insists that divine revelation reaches the human spirit "in a variety of ways, in a multiplicity of languages," that "one truth comes to expression in many ways of understanding."[58] In that same context, he adds: "No word is God's last word, no word is God's ultimate word."[59]

One of the things that Heschel teaches us by his attitude toward religious diversity is to be open to the revelation of God wherever it may be discerned, and that such openness is an expression of trust in the God of our tradition who transcends all traditions. God's revelation may be found in many places in this world, including in the context of different religious traditions, particularly wherever justice and love are fostered. Thus, for example, while "a false prophet" is someone who "proclaims words that add and strengthen hatred," Heschel claims that "a true prophet" is someone who "utters words that enhance the power of love, enhance the power of justice."[60]

Redemption through a Variety of Ways

It is clear from the above that, for Heschel, the purpose or end of divine revelation is the world's redemption. And just as Judaism always has recognized that righteous Gentiles have a share in "the World to Come," so has it acknowledged the fact that people apart from Judaism can—indeed, they must—do their part to help God redeem this world. But here, again, Heschel goes further than his tradition by suggesting that various religions are necessary for redemption to reach its climax.

In the context where he asserts that "diversity of religions is the will of God," Heschel asks: "Does not the task of preparing the Kingdom of God require a diversity of talents, a variety of rituals, soul-searching as well as opposition?"[61] If this is so, does it not follow that peoples of various religions have been chosen by God for various tasks? Speaking specifically about Christianity, Heschel says: "The Jewish attitude enables us to acknowledge the presence of a divine plan in the role of Christianity within the history of redemption."[62] Then, commenting on views about both Christianity and Islam expounded by two great medieval Jewish authorities, Yehudah Halevi and Maimonides, Heschel says approvingly: "Christianity and Islam, far from being accidents of history or purely human phenomena, are regarded as part of God's design for the redemption of all."[63]

Notice that Heschel speaks of a *history* of redemption. From his Jewish perspective, redemption is not only an event that will occur at the end of history but a process that may go on all the time—enhanced or retarded by human deeds. The goal of this process is the reign of God, which is the unity of humanity and the world in communion with God. Here, again, Heschel draws his inspiration from the *Sh'ma*: "It is only in the mirror of divine unity that we may behold the unity of all."[64]

But the unity of humanity and world is now more of a task than a condition. "Creature is detached from the Creator, and the universe is in a state of spiritual disorder," writes Heschel. "The goal of all efforts is to bring about the restitution of the unity of God and world. The restoration of that unity is a constant process and its accomplishment will be the essence of messianic redemption."[65]

But how is this to be achieved? Heschel's answer: "Love is what brings the world forward" toward redemption.[66] In reflecting on the Arab-Israeli conflict, for example, Heschel writes: "The choice is to love together or to perish together."[67] And this same principle applies to the entire human race. Heschel quotes with approval the words of another great rabbi, Abraham Isaac Kook (1865–1935), the first Ashkenazic chief rabbi of Palestine in 1921: "It will be love without cause that will save Israel and all mankind."[68]

From Heschel's perspective, religions can be considered valid to the extent that they inspire people to live by way of love. Even if their avowed goal is not redemption of the world as taught by Judaism, religions that inspire genuine love do advance the world toward redemption and thus may be said to be divinely inspired.

Faith in God vis-à-vis Beliefs and Doctrines about God

To speak about that which is avowed is to speak of belief and creed. Heschel frequently refers to his work as "depth theology," the effort at religious self-understanding by way of an exploration of "the depth of faith, the substratum out of which belief arises."[69] He calls this task "depth theology" in order to distinguish it from what is often meant by "theology." Theology deals with the *content* of belief; depth theology deals with the *act* of faith as well as with the experiences that precede and nurture faith. Accordingly, Heschel distinguishes between faith and belief as well as between faith and creed, the doctrinal content of belief. An examination of these distinctions will help us better understand Heschel's appreciation of religious diversity as the will of God.

Faith in God and Beliefs about God

"Faith is not the same as belief, not the same as the attitude of regarding something as true."[70] Belief is a mental assent to a proposition or to an alleged fact, the truth of which is acknowledged on the basis of authority or evidence. Faith, on the other hand, is far more than an attitude of the mind. "Faith is an act of the whole person, of mind, will, and heart," writes Heschel. "Faith is *sensitivity*, *understanding*, *engagement*, and *attachment*."[71] As such, "faith is not the assent to an idea, but the consent to God."[72]

When we say that we "believe in" someone or something we may mean that we have faith in that person or that reality, that we trust in, rely upon, and strive to be faithful to the object of our belief. But such *believing in* someone or something is quite different from *believing that* someone or something exists or that a proposition is true.[73] Believing that something exists or is true is an act of the intellect; believing in something is a matter of faith and as such is an act of the whole person, not just the intellect.

"Faith is a relation to God," writes Heschel; "belief a relation to an idea or a dogma."[74] Belief, therefore, refers to what is known or comprehended; faith refers to a reality that transcends human comprehension. An idea, even an idea about God, is comprehensible; but the reality itself, especially the reality of God, is something "we apprehend but cannot comprehend."[75]

Judaism, like other religions, calls for belief—beliefs about God and other basic teachings—but it is faith, not belief, that is primary. "It is by faith and love of God that find expression in deeds that we live as Jews," writes Heschel. "Not the confession of belief, but the active acceptance of the kingship of God and its order is the central demand of Judaism. . . . Thus our relation to God cannot be expressed in a belief but rather in the accepting of an order that determines all of life."[76] Faith presupposes belief, but belief is no substitute for faith, and faith is not reducible to belief. If belief is separated from faith it is a spiritually meaningless intellectual assent. And if faith does not formulate its belief it is, no matter how spiritually meaningful, an unintelligible act. Seeking intelligibility, faith attempts to declare its belief in the form of doctrines or creed.

Faith in God and Doctrines about God

One of the things that characterizes Judaism and is among the principal reasons for Heschel's appreciation of religious diversity is "the primacy of faith over creed."[77] "The soul rarely knows how to raise its deeper secrets to discursive levels of the mind. We must not, therefore, equate the act of faith with its expression."[78] A creed of doctrines is an expression of faith, not to be confused with faith itself, which, as we have seen, is an act of the whole person, involving insight, trust, and fidelity. Doctrines are acts of the mind, affirmations of truths perceived in faith. On the relationship between them, Heschel writes: "Faith becomes a dogma or a doctrine when crystallized in an opinion. In other words, what is expressed and taught as a creed is but the adaptation of the uncommon spirit to the common mind. . . . Faith is an act of spiritual audacity, while in employing terms we necessarily come to terms with our desire for intellectual security, for steadiness, tranquility."[79]

Given this relationship between faith and creed, Heschel calls creed "the diminutive of faith."[80] Moreover, he points out that there are "many strata of faith for which we have no dogmas" and that dogmas can even "stand in the way of authentic faith" if they are presumed to capture its fullness.[81] But, if properly employed as allusions rather than as descriptions, dogmas can preserve, communicate, and even illumine the insights of faith. "The adequacy of dogmas depends on whether they claim to formulate or to allude; in the first case they flaunt and fail, in the second they indicate and illumine," writes Heschel. "To be adequate they must retain a telescopic relation to the theme to which they refer, must point to the mysteries of God rather than picture them. All they can do is indicate a way, not mark an end, of thinking. Unless they serve as humble signposts on the way dogmas are obstacles."[82]

So while Heschel recognizes the value of dogmas, he also points out "the danger of dogmas [that] lies in their tendency to serve as *vicarious faith*, as if all we had to do were to accept on authority a fixed set of principles without the necessity of searching for a way of faith."[83] Heschel is wary of the human tendency to idolize dogmas, to serve them rather than the God to whom they are meant to testify. Thus, he reminds us that "an idea or a theory of God can easily become a substitute for God, impressive to the mind when God as a living reality is absent from the soul."[84] In short, "God may be lost in our creed."[85]

Moreover, when the value of creed is inflated, people of different creeds often replace faith with suspicion, prejudice, and inquisition. But when the primacy of faith is acknowledged, Heschel believes that people espousing different creeds are more likely to unite in the search for truth. With this distinction between faith and creed in mind, and speaking of "different religious traditions," Heschel claims that "our individual moments of faith are mere waves in the endless ocean of mankind's reaching out for God, where all formulations and articulations appear as understatements."[86] So whatever Heschel thinks of various creeds, with this perspective he is able to perceive authenticity in the faith that is fostered by various religions.

It is important to note that while Heschel makes a distinction between faith and creed, he does not present them as independent of each other. On the contrary, for him, religious doctrines are meant to "crystallize" the insights of faith, to "telescope" its mysteries. One of the primary goals of religious existence, according to Heschel, is to keep alive the polarity of faith and creed and to maintain a proper balance between them. Without creed, faith is vague and private. But "the overgrowth of creed may smash and seal the doom of faith," says Heschel. "A minimum of creed and a maximum of faith is the ideal synthesis."[87]

And while in one instance Heschel says "there are many creeds, but only one universal faith,"[88] generally his writings indicate an awareness on his part of the uniqueness of various experiences of faith and not just expressions of it. His distinction between processes and events, which we discussed in chapter 2, is germane to this point. In speaking of different revelatory events, Heschel suggests that there are different experiences of the divine disclosure, and hence different experiences of faith in response to different revelations. Thus, Heschel's speaking of "one universal faith" appears to contradict a perspective of his that he usually conveys in his writings.

Nevertheless, while Heschel appears to realize that there are distinctive experiences of faith and not only distinctive doctrines that distinguish different religions, he does believe and emphasize that at the level of faith people of various traditions have more in common than their different doctrines indicate. For example, while Judaism and Christianity foster different though related types of religious experience, Heschel suggests that what is peculiar to each religion is not what is most essential to each: "The supreme issue is today not the *halacha* for the Jew or the Church for the Christian—but the premise underlying both religions, namely, whether there is a *pathos*, a divine reality concerned with the destiny of man which mysteriously impinges upon history; the supreme issue is whether we are alive or dead to the challenge and the expectation of the living God."[89]

While both a Jew and a Christian may discern and respond to the challenge and expectation of the living God, each does so differently: a Jew by way of the Torah in the context of the Jewish people's covenantal life, a Christian through Jesus Christ in the context of the church's covenantal life. Each has a different religious experience, but what is more important is that the experiences of both have to do with the same living God. So while their respective creeds divide them, they are united in faith. "What divides us?" asks Heschel. "We disagree in law and creed, in commitments which lie at the very heart of our religious existence. . . . What unites us? A commitment to the Hebrew Bible as Holy Scripture. Faith in the Creator, the God of Abraham . . . sensitivity to the sanctity of life and to the involvement of God in history . . . and so much more."[90]

But Heschel's perspective on religious diversity is much more radical than his perceiving a unity in faith between Jews and Christians. It is even more radical than, as we saw above, his acknowledging "Christianity and Islam . . . as part of God's design," for he also speaks of a "community of faith" that extends far beyond the monotheistic world.[91] "The intuition of God is universal, yet there is hardly a universal form—with few possible exceptions—to express it. . . . If uniformity and impeccability of expression were the mark of authenticity, such divergence . . . would refute the assumption of the reality of the mystery. The fact, however, is that opinions about God throughout history do not show a greater variety than, for example, opinions about the nature of the world."[92] Heschel even finds biblical support for his view:

> From the rising of the sun to its setting My name is great among the nations, and in every place incense is offered to My name, and a pure offering; for My name is great among the nations, says the Lord of Hosts (Malachi 1:11).
>
> This statement refers undoubtedly to the contemporaries of the prophet. But who were these worshippers of One God? At the time of Malachi there was hardly a large number of proselytes. Yet the statement declares: All those who worship their gods do not know it, but they are really worshipping Me.

It seems that the prophet proclaims that men all over the world, though they confess different conceptions of God are really worshipping One God . . . though they may not be aware of it.[93]

For Heschel, even those religions whose rituals would by biblical standards be considered idolatrous may be fostering communion with God. The error of religious people whose rituals are outside the framework of monotheistic religion is not necessarily in their sense of mystery or transcendence but, according to Heschel, in their expressions of it.[94]

But Heschel is well aware that monotheists also often make errors in the way they speak of God. In any case, and more important, Heschel's point in employing the quotation from Malachi is not to brand non-monotheists as idol worshipers but, on the contrary, to suggest that even in the Bible there appears to be support for the idea that non-monotheists, who in the biblical worldview are considered idolaters, may, in the context of their rituals, somehow be honoring the God beyond their gods—and thereby cultivating their relationship with this one and only true God.

To be sure, Heschel shows no interest in branding non-monotheistic religions as idolatrous. Whenever he writes about idolatry, it is to condemn as idolatrous our living as if something other than God—including an expression of monotheistic religion—is equal to or more important than God. Recall Heschel's words cited in the first section of this chapter: "Religion is a means, not an end. It becomes idolatrous when regarded as an end in itself." Here Heschel is not excluding monotheistic religion. And, in case there is any doubt, in another of his statements, also cited above, by speaking of "our faith" Heschel is explicitly referring to monotheism: "To rely on our faith would be idol-worship. We have only the right to rely on God." And just as explicitly: "Manasseh, we are told, placed an idol in the Temple. Is it not possible that there are idols in our homes, in our minds, in our temples?"[95] Yes, those of us whose creed is monotheistic may, at the deeper level of faith, be idolatrous, and Heschel calls upon us "to reject as vulgar and destructive certain values that our own people cherish and worship!"[96]

Clearly, for Heschel, the issue of genuine faith versus idolatry has to do with the issue of our values. Do we cherish values that are truly godly, that reflect the love and compassion of God, or do we cling to ungodly values more than to God and what God expects of us? Monotheism at the level of creed has to do with what we say we believe; monotheism at the level of faith has to do with the values we hold dear and by which we live.

Just as Heschel insists that people may know God "unknowingly" and fail to know God "when insisting upon knowing," he clearly believes that people's actions, regardless of their creed, may or may not be ways of living in harmony with God, ways of worshiping God. In the context of writing about religious diversity, Heschel cites the following ancient rabbinic text: "I call heaven and earth to witness that the Holy Spirit rests upon each person, Jew or Gentile, man or woman, master or slave, in consonance with his [or her] deeds."[97] Harold Kasimow is to the point: "For Heschel, it is less important what religious path people follow than that they show compassion for their fellow humans."[98]

"What is an idol?" asks Heschel. And here is his answer: "*Any god who is mine but not yours*, any god concerned with me but not with you, *is an idol.*" And, after offering this definition of an idol, the very first example of idolatry that Heschel gives is "*racial or religious bigotry* [that] must be recognized for what it is: *satanism, blasphemy.*"[99] He goes on to say that "worship without compassion is . . . an abomination," that "an act of violence is an act of desecration," and that to be arrogant toward other people "is to be blasphemous toward God."[100]

People in all religions, even those who confess monotheism, can commit such blasphemy or idolatry, just as all people can by their good deeds give homage to God. And, in Heschel's view, all religions, not just monotheistic religions, have validity to the extent that they foster good deeds. "What all religions have in common," he claims, is an insistence that the dignity of human beings is in their "power of compassion" and their "capacity for sacrifice."[101] We may know that "diversity of religions is the will of God" precisely because we are able to witness a diversity of religious ways of promoting these moral virtues, of fostering human dignity, and of thereby honoring the ultimate reality that we who are monotheists call God.

Abbreviations

The following are the abbreviations for Heschel's books used in the notes.
Full bibliographical information is supplied in the bibliography.

BGM   *Between God and Man*

EL   *The Earth Is the Lord's*

GSM   *God In Search of Man*

HT   *Heavenly Torah*

IE   *Israel: An Echo of Eternity*

IF   *The Insecurity of Freedom*

IN   *The Ineffable Name of God*

MG   *Moral Grandeur and Spiritual Audacity*

MNA   *Man Is Not Alone*

MQG   *Man's Quest for God*

P   *The Prophets*

PT   *A Passion for Truth*

S   *The Sabbath*

WM   *Who Is Man?*

NOTES

Preface, pages ix–xi

1. *WM*, 71.
2. *GSM*, 162.

Introduction, pages 1–12

1. Robert McAfee Brown, "Abraham Heschel: A Passion for Sincerity," *Christianity and Crisis* (December 10, 1973): 257–58.

2. Jacob Y. Teshima, "My Memory of Professor Abraham Joshua Heschel," *Conservative Judaism* (Fall 1973): 80.

3. Edward K. Kaplan, "Form and Content in Abraham J. Heschel's Poetic Style," *Central Conference of American Rabbis* (April 1971): 29.

4. *PT*, xiv.

5. *PT*, xiv.

6. Abraham Joshua Heschel, *Kotzk: In gerangl far emesdikeit* [*Kotzk: The Struggle for Integrity*], Yiddish, 2 vols. (Tel-Aviv: Hamenora Publishing House, 1973), 10. This quotation was translated and cited by Harold Kasimow in *The Divine-Human Encounter: A Study of Abraham Joshua Heschel* (Washington DC: University Press of America, 1979), 3.

7. Heschel, quoted from an interview with Jack D. Spiro held in October 1971, in Jack D. Spiro, "Rabbi Abraham Joshua Heschel: An Appreciation," *Religious Education* (March–April 1973): 220.

8. Fritz A. Rothschild, "Introduction," *BGM*, 7–8. Rothschild's statement includes a quotation from *EL*, 56.

9. Edward K. Kaplan and Samuel H. Dresner, *Abraham Joshua Heschel: Prophetic Witness* (New Haven and London: Yale University Press, 1998), 47.

10. Ibid.

11. Fritz A. Rothschild, "Architect and Herald of a New Theology," *America* (March 10, 1973): 211. Because Heschel's theology of pathos challenges classical metaphysical theology, it is understandable that, in return, it has received its share of criticism. See my essay "Heschel's Theology of Divine Pathos," in *Abraham Joshua Heschel: Exploring His Life and Thought*, ed. John C. Merkle (New York and London: Macmillan, 1985), 66–83,

in which I defend Heschel's theology of pathos against the most sustained criticism it has received.

12. Rothschild, "Introduction," *BGM*, 24 in first edition; 25 in revised edition. See also Fritz A. Rothschild, "Varieties of Heschelian Thought," in *Abraham Joshua Heschel: Exploring His Life and Thought*, 88–89: "The key to Heschel's thought is not Being, but Concern for being. . . . Aristotle's Unmoved Mover must give way to the Bible's Most Moved Mover, the God of pathos who stands in a dynamic and reciprocal relationship to creation."

13. *MG*, 156.

14. Susannah Heschel, "Introduction," *MG*, xxii.

15. *PT*, 258–59.

16. *IN*, 31.

17. *IN*, 45.

18. Samuel H. Dresner, "Introduction: Heschel as a Hasidic Scholar," in Abraham J. Heschel, *The Circle of the Baal Shem Tov: Studies in Hasidism*, ed. Samuel H. Dresner (Chicago and London: University of Chicago Press, 1985), viii.

19. Rothschild, "Introduction," *BGM*, 8.

20. Kaplan, *Abraham Joshua Heschel: Prophetic Witness*, 202 and 206.

21. Ibid., 236.

22. Ibid., 252.

23. Ibid., 257.

24. *MG*, 117.

25. Reinhold Niebuhr, quoted by Byron Sherwin, "Abraham Joshua Heschel," *The Torch* (Spring 1969): 7.

26. Heschel, *The Quest for Certainty in Saadia's Philosophy* (New York: Philip Feldheim, 1944), 2.

27. *IF*, 246.

28. J. A. Sanders, "An Apostle to the Gentiles," *Conservative Judaism* (Fall 1973): 62.

29. Moshe Starkman, "Abraham Joshua Heschel: The Jewish Writer and Thinker," *Conservative Judaism* (Fall 1973): 75.

30. W. D. Davies, "Conscience, Scholar, Witness," *America* (March 10, 1973): 215.

31. *IF*, 248.

32. Rothschild, "Architect and Herald of a New Theology," 211.

33. A later version of this address was published as "The Meaning of this War," *Hebrew Union College Bulletin* (March 1943): 1–2, 18; reprinted in *MQG*, 147–51.

34. *IF*, 86.

35. Martin Luther King Jr., in "Conversation with Martin Luther King," *Conversation Judaism* (Spring 1968): 2; King was interviewed by Rabbi Everett Gendler on March 25, 1968, ten days before he was murdered.

36. Brown, "Abraham Heschel: A Passion for Sincerity," 256. See also Brown's essay "Heschel's Social Ethics," in *Abraham Joshua Heschel: Exploring His Life and Thought*, 123–41, where he also discusses Heschel's response to the Vietnam War.

37. Heschel, "The Moral Outrage of Vietnam," in *Vietnam: Crisis of Conscience*, eds. Robert McAfee Brown, Abraham J. Heschel, and Michael Novak (New York: Herder and Herder, 1967), 49.

38. John C. Bennett, "Agent of God's Compassion," *America* (March 10, 1973): 206.

39. Edward K. Kaplan, *Spiritual Radical: Abraham Joshua Heschel in America* (New Haven and London: Yale University Press, 2007), 296, 306.

40. Reuven Kimelman, "Abraham Joshua Heschel (1907–1972)," *Response: A Contemporary Jewish Review* (Winter 1972–73): 18.

41. *IF*, 272–73.

42. Fritz A. Rothschild, "Abraham Joshua Heschel (1907–1972): Theologian and Scholar," in *American Jewish Yearbook*, 74, eds. Morris Fine and Milton Himmelfarb (Philadelphia: Jewish Publication Society of America, 1973), 535.

43. Brown, "Abraham Heschel: A Passion for Sincerity," 257.

44. *MG*, 244.

Chapter One, pages 13–32

1. *GSM*, 33.
2. See *MNA*, 3 and *GSM*, 33–34.
3. *GSM*, 39.
4. *MNA*, 4; repeated in *GSM*, 39.
5. *IF*, 41–42.
6. *WM*, 86.
7. *IF*, 47.
8. *MNA*, 22.
9. Alfred North Whitehead, *Science and the Modern World* (New York: Macmillan, 1926), 286.
10. *MNA*, 22.
11. *WM*, 66; *IF*, 259; *MQG*, 39; *IF*, 248; *MQG*, 105.
12. *MG*, 238.
13. *MNA*, 39.
14. *WM*, 46.
15. *MNA*, 21.
16. *MNA*, 4–5.
17. *GSM*, 58; see also *GSM*, 34, 160.
18. *WM*, 77.
19. *WM*, 31.
20. *GSM*, 54.
21. *GSM*, 161.
22. *GSM*, 210.
23. *MNA*, 30–31.
24. *GSM*, 59.
25. *GSM*, 114–15.
26. *GSM*, 107.
27. *GSM*, 57–58.
28. *MNA*, 46.
29. *MNA*, 44.
30. *MNA*, 16.
31. *MNA*, 48, 47, 48.
32. *MNA*, 202–3.
33. *WM*, 60.

34. *WM*, 111.
35. *GSM*, 89.
36. *WM*, 73.
37. *WM*, 76; *MG*, 330.
38. *MNA*, 78.
39. *MNA*, 227.
40. *GSM*, 114.
41. *MNA*, 253.
42. *IN*, 75.
43. *MNA*, 78.
44. *MNA*, 289.
45. *MNA*, 76.
46. *GSM*, 110
47. *WM*, 73.
48. *WM*, 64.
49. *WM*, 74.
50. *WM*, 69; *MG*, 251.
51. See *GSM*, 158.
52. *GSM*, 250.
53. *MNA*, 73.
54. *MNA*, 61, 65, 64.
55. *MNA*, 72.
56. *MNA*, 70.
57. *MNA*, 226.
58. *MNA*, 112.
59. *GSM*, 161.
60. *MNA*, 120, 123.
61. *IF*, 95.
62. *IF*, 86.
63. *MNA*, 94, 109.
64. *MNA*, 112, 113.
65. *GSM*, 162.
66. *WM*, 71.
67. *MNA*, 140.
68. *GSM*, 162.
69. *MG*, 261.
70. *GSM*, 159.
71. *GSM*, 158.
72. *IF*, 3.
73. *WM*, 108.
74. *MNA*, 284.
75. *MNA*, 144.
76. *MNA*, 282.
77. *GSM*, 158, 138.
78. *MNA*, 284.
79. *MNA*, 147.
80. *MNA*, 149; *MG*, 238; *GSM*, 289.

81. *MNA*, 225–26, 237.

82. *MNA*, 145.

83. *MNA*, 150.

84. *MG*, 295; *MNA*, 284.

85. *P*, 266.

86. *GSM*, 137.

87. *MNA*, 84.

88. *GSM*, 121. This is a slight revision of what Heschel had already written in *MNA*, 84.

89. *MNA*, 136.

90. See *MNA*, 137–39.

91. See *MNA*, 143.

92. *MNA*, 135.

93. *GSM*, 181–82.

94. *MNA*, 142.

95. *MNA*, 145.

96. *MNA*, 12.

97. *WM*, 70.

98. *WM*, 71.

99. *WM*, 71.

100. *WM*, 71.

101. *WM*, 91.

102. *GSM*, 102.

103. *GSM*, 110; see also *MNA*, 54–55: "The idea of a supreme designer may serve as a source of intellectual security in our search for the design, law and order of the universe. However . . . is order the utmost that divine wisdom could produce? We are more anxious to know whether there is a God of justice than to learn whether there is a God of order. Is there a God who collects the tears, who honors hope and rewards the ordeals of the guiltless? Or should we assume that the empires of thought, the saintly goals, the harmonies and sacrificial deeds of the honest and the meek are nothing but images painted upon the surface of an ocean?"

104. *WM*, 91–92.

105. See, e.g., *IE*, 131; *MG*, 159–60, 260, 291, 332; *MNA*, 119, 153; *P*, 240–41; *WM*, 90.

Chapter 2, pages 33–54

1. *GSM*, 200, 202.

2. *GSM*, 209; repeated in *P*, 431 and *WM*, 42.

3. *P*, 431.

4. *IF*, 182; see also *MG*, 245: "No word is God's last word, no word is God's ultimate word."

5. *P*, 436.

6. *GSM*, 207.

7. *IN*, 195.

8. See *GSM*, 155.

9. *IE*, 130.

10. *IN*, 33.

11. *MG*, 267.

12. *GSM*, 81.

13. *GSM*, 255.

14. *IN*, 69.

15. *GSM*, 188.

16. *GSM*, 174.

17. See *GSM*, 169–70.

18. See *GSM*, 171.

19. *GSM*, 173.

20. *P*, 227.

21. *WM*, 77.

22. *GSM*, 173.

23. *GSM*, 174.

24. *GSM*, 189.

25. *GSM*, 184.

26. *GSM*, 185.

27. *GSM*, 178–79.

28. *IF*, 177; see also *MNA, 168*.

29. *GSM*, 187.

30. *GSM*, 180.

31. *GSM*, 183.

32. *GSM*, 252.

33. *GSM*, 243.

34. *GSM*, 252.

35. *GSM*, 252.

36. *GSM*, 232.

37. *GSM*, 250; see also *HT*, 668: "You cannot grasp the matter of the 'Torah from Heaven' unless you feel the heaven in the Torah."

38. *GSM*, 265.

39. *GSM*, 260.

40. See *GSM*, 261.

41. *GSM*, 264.

42. *GSM*, 261.

43. *GSM*, 268.

44. *GSM*, 268, 269.

45. *MG*, 160; see also *P*, 222, where Heschel refers to "the divine pathos" as "a central category in prophetic theology."

46. *P*, 219.

47. *P*, 220.

48. *P*, 277.

49. See *P*, 226.

50. *P*, 224.

51. *P*, 259.

52. *P*, 151.

53. Alfred North Whitehead, *Process and Reality: An Essay in Cosmology* (New York: Macmillan, 1929), 532.

54. *P*, 260.

55. *P*, 262.

56. Whitehead, *Process and Reality*, 521.

57. *P*, 277.

58. Thomas Aquinas, *Summa Theologiae* I, Question 13, Article 7.

59. *MNA*, 244.

60. *P*, 248.

61. Edmond La B. Cherbonnier, "Heschel as a Religious Thinker," *Conservative Judaism* (Fall 1968): 33.

62. *P*, 250.

63. *P*, 316.

64. *P*, 258.

65. *P*, 238.

66. *P*, 224.

67. *P*, 256.

68. *P*, 225.

69. *P*, 201.

70. *P*, 315.

71. *MG*, 160. As might be expected of anyone whose writing career spanned more than four decades, Heschel appears not to have been entirely consistent on some of the issues he addressed throughout his career, and this seems to be the case concerning his reflections on the issue of divine power. See Alexander Even-Chen's helpful article, "God's Omnipotence and Presence in Abraham Joshua Heschel's Philosophy," *Shofar: An Interdisciplinary Journal of Jewish Studies* (Fall 2007): 41-71, in which Even-Chen explores "Heschel's changing perspective on the matters of the almightiness and of the potency of God throughout his lifetime" (41). Even-Chen suggests that in Heschel's earliest writings, particularly his poems published in *The Ineffable Name of God*, Heschel assumes God's omnipotence and, in some of those poems, rails against God for not intervening in the world as he assumes God has the power to do. By the 1940s, says Even-Chen, "Heschel sees God's power waning before his eyes" (49) and "begins to stress that God is not almighty" (52) and "no longer demands that God intervene" (53). Even-Chen suggests that this view of his persists until Israel's "victory in the war [the Six Day War of 1967] led Heschel to the renewed belief in a God of history" (69), i.e., by which Even-Chen means a God who, because omnipotent, is able to rule history, which he suggests is the perspective with which Heschel begins *IE* before "further on in the book Heschel recants [this belief in divine omnipotence] and reiterates the notion that God is indeed powerless" (69). As helpful as Even-Chen's article is, I think he is wrong to suggest that the Six Day War caused Heschel to return to a belief in divine omnipotence. In fact, I am not sure that Heschel's early poems, some of which call upon God to intervene, indicate that even in his early adulthood Heschel believed in divine omnipotence. To call upon God to intervene in the world, and to rail against God for not intervening as hoped for, does not necessarily indicate a belief in divine omnipotence; it may only imply a belief in divine power, even if that power is in some sense understood to be limited by God's creation. So also, Heschel's rejection of the idea of divine omnipotence should not be interpreted to mean, as Even Chen suggests, that Heschel held that "God is indeed powerless." The options are not simply omnipotence and powerlessness. Clearly, all the while that Heschel rejects the idea of divine omnipotence he nonetheless believes that

God has power, just not—having created creatures with degrees of power—all the power, i.e., not the power to exercise power totally independent of the cooperation of creatures. Concerning Heschel's alleged return to a belief in divine omnipotence, I do not see anything in *IE* that suggests this. The fact that, as cited by Even-Chen (70), Heschel calls God "the Lord of history [who] does not slumber or sleep" (*IE* 48) does not mean that Heschel now thinks God is omnipotent. When rejecting the belief in divine omnipotence, Heschel does not, as Even-Chen suggests he does, reject the belief that God is the Lord of history. Heschel never suggests that God has to control history in order to be the Lord of history. What he regularly implies is that God is the Lord of history because God has revealed the goal of history and the way to reach that goal. For Heschel to say (poetically) that God "does not slumber or sleep" in no way suggests that he believes God controls history. In fact, in the very book in question, as I am about to indicate in the text, Heschel suggests that God's presence in history should not be understood as God's dominance of history (see *IE*, 131). I agree that throughout his career, and at times even in the same book, Heschel made statements about God's presence and power that do not appear entirely consistent with each other, but, in my reading of Heschel, he persisted, if not all the way from the early 1930s, at least from the 1940s until his last writings, in rejecting the idea of divine omnipotence. Even-Chen acknowledges that "two years after the victory [of the Six Day War] Heschel published an article about Jewish theology in which he restates the limits of God's might," but his final suggestion (71) that Heschel thought Israel's victory in the Six Day War indicated divine omnipotence is completely unfounded. For Heschel, the actualization of God's power in the world depends on the cooperation of human beings, including the people of Israel, but he never suggests that people either make or unmake divine omnipotence (which would be a contradictory claim, as omnipotence by its very nature could not be dependent on any other power), but that they simply cooperate with or obstruct divine ways, including the ways of God's power—which he does not think of as omnipotence, i.e., as power to do whatever God desires regardless of the cooperation of creatures.

72. See, e.g., *IE*, 131.

73. *MG*, 332.

74. *MG*, 260.

75. *HT*, 121. One has to be especially careful about suggesting that statements made by Heschel in *HT* actually reflect his perspective. This is because in this book, far more than in his other books, Heschel summarizes different interpretations usually without indicating his preferences. (In fact, while one of the main purposes of nearly every other one of Heschel's books is to argue in favor of one or more theological perspectives, the main purpose of *HT* is to demonstrate the diversity of interpretations within rabbinic literature on various issues concerning revelation.) But at times Heschel's preferences do come through, and I am confident that I am accurate when suggesting this is the case.

76. *P*, 240–41.

77. *P*, 214.

78. The theme of God's need for human beings is prevalent throughout Heschel's writings. See, e.g., *MNA*, 215, 241–48; *WM*, 73–75; *IF*, 8, 67, 97; *PT*, 300–301. When Heschel speaks of God's need for human beings he of course does not suggest that God's existence is dependent upon human beings but that God's redemptive activity requires human cooperation. God is ontologically self-sufficient but not soteriologically self-sufficient. And the only sense in which God is ontologically self-sufficient is that the

divine being is neither derived from (created by) nor dependent on (sustained by) any other being. God is not ontologically self-sufficient in the Aristotelian sense that the divine being is "resting purely within itself," unmoved by the plight of creatures and hence apathetic. On the contrary, as discussed above, God wills not to be alone and is intimately affected by the doings and sufferings of creatures.

79. According to Heschel, "the prophet may be characterized as a *homo sympathetikos*," as a person who has "sympathetic solidarity with God" as a result of being "moved by the pathos of God" (*P*, 308, 313, 314).

80. *GSM*, 274.

81. *GSM*, 27.

82. *GSM*, 185.

83. *GSM*, 273.

84. *GSM*, 274.

85. *GSM*, 239. See also *HT*, 663: "The giving of the written Torah is the beginning, not the end, of Torah."

86. *GSM*, 274. See also *HT*, 663: "No single generation can make constructions for *all* generations. But in every generation the officers of Israel construct and innovate and thus add to those who preceded them."

87. *GSM*, 274–75. See also *HT*, 663 where Heschel quotes Leviticus Rabbah 11:7, "Without Sages there is no Torah"; and *HT*, 665 where he writes: "The Sages often add to and detract from the Torah, such as when they added a day to the festivals in the Diaspora, or abolished the blowing of the Shofar and the taking of the Lulav when the holiday coincides with the Sabbath."

88. *GSM*, 273.

89. *GSM*, 272–73.

90. *MNA*, 164–65.

91. *GSM*, 288.

92. See *GSM*, 288.

93. *IF*, 198.

94. *GSM*, 307.

95. *IF*, 220; *GSM*, 338.

96. *GSM*, 299.

97. *MQG*, 102.

98. See *GSM*, 272, 270.

99. *MG*, 197.

100. *MQG*, 93.

101. *MQG*, 94.

102. *MQG*, 103.

103. *EL*, 62–63.

104. *MNA*, 266–67.

105. *GSM*, 307.

106. *GSM*, 356.

107. *MG*, 194.

108. *MG*, 194.

109. *MG*, 194, 195.

110. *MG*, 194.

111. *MG*, 198.

Chapter 3, pages 55–73

1. *GSM*, 30.
2. *MQG*, 63.
3. *GSM*, 40.
4. *MQG*, 63.
5. *GSM*, 349.
6. *MNA*, 37.
7. *MNA*, 36.
8. *WM*, 82.
9. *WM*, 78–79. Fritz Rothschild's interpretation ("Introduction," *BGM*, 11–12 in first edition; 12 in revised edition) of Heschel's approach to this contrast between wonder and accepting reality at face value is instructive: "Acceptance stops with whatever is perceived and sees no good reason for going beyond it. The object is admitted as a given (datum) and that is all there is to it. Wonder, on the other hand, is an attitude which, far from being set at ease by a fact, takes it as a stimulus which points beyond what is immediately given."
10. *MNA*, 63.
11. *MNA*, 12.
12. *WM*, 87. Wonder as radical amazement is a recurring theme in Heschel's writings, and chapter 2 of *MNA* is titled "Radical Amazement." On the distinction between "ultimate wonder" as radical amazement and "rational wonder" as curiosity, see *GSM*, 45–46.
13. *GSM*, 99.
14. *GSM*, 110.
15. *MNA*, 44.
16. *GSM*, 77.
17. Although Heschel does not refer to Rudolf Otto's classic work *The Idea of the Holy*, trans. John W. Harvey (Oxford and New York: Oxford University Press, 1958), his writings show that he, like Otto, views mystery as both overwhelming and fascinating.
18. *MNA*, 27.
19. *GSM*, 78.
20. *GSM*, 74.
21. *GSM*, 74, 73.
22. *MNA*, 130.
23. *GSM*, 75.
24. *GSM*, 75.
25. *MQG*, 59.
26. *MQG*, 88.
27. *WM*, 116.
28. *MG*, 257.
29. *MQG*, 55.
30. *MQG*, 46.
31. *MQG*, 82; repeated in *IF*, 245.
32. *GSM*, 95.
33. *MNA*, 41.
34. *IN*, 143.

35. *MQG*, 39.
36. *MQG*, 41.
37. *MQG*, 33, 40.
38. *IF*, 244; *IN*, 161.
39. *MNA*, 75; *IF*, 245.
40. *MG*, 263.
41. *MQG*, 60.
42. *GSM*, 290.
43. *S*, 8.
44. *GSM*, 200; *IE*, 233.
45. *GSM*, 211, 215.
46. *IF*, 251.
47. *MQG*, 25; *IF*, 260.
48. *IF*, 249.
49. *MQG*, 33.
50. *MQG*, 28.
51. *MQG*, 30.
52. *MQG*, 47.
53. *MQG*, 29, 30.
54. *GSM*, 408.
55. *MQG*, 28.
56. *MQG*, 31.
57. *MQG*, 32.
58. *MG*, 257, 258.
59. *IF*, 42.
60. *PT*, 56.
61. *IF*, 42.
62. *IF*, 42.
63. *IF*, 237.
64. *IF*, 236.
65. *IF*, 237.
66. *IF*, 237.
67. *IF*, 50.
68. *IF*, 54.
69. *IF*, 39–40.
70. *IF*, 21; repeated in *IF*, 215.
71. *IF*, 20.
72. *WM*, 37.
73. *MQG*, 112.
74. *IF*, 192.
75. *IF*, 226.
76. *EL*, 54.
77. *IF*, 42.
78. *WM*, 44.
79. *IF*, 60.
80. *IF*, 73.
81. *IF*, 231.

82. *IF*, 59.

83. *IF*, 50, 84.

84. *IF*, 42–43.

85. *IF*, 78.

86. *EL*, 42–44.

87. *PT*, 63.

88. *PT*, 164.

89. *PT*, 164.

90. *IF*, 42.

91. *GSM*, 384; *MG*, 197.

92. *PT*, 62. The quote is from *Sayings of the Fathers,* III, 12. See also *MG*, 196: "An accepted statement of rabbinic tradition is that not study but the deed is the most important thing."

93. *IF*, 87.

94. *P*, 195.

95. *P*, 195.

96. *MG*, 261.

97. *GSM*, 296.

98. *GSM*, 295.

99. *GSM*, 345.

100. *GSM*, 296–97.

101. *GSM*, 297.

102. *GSM*, 284.

103. *GSM*, 282.

104. *MNA*, 139, 142.

105. *GSM*, 312.

106. *GSM*, 345. See also *GSM*, 404: "Purity of motivation is the goal; constancy of action is the way. . . . It is the act that teaches us the meaning of the act. The way to pure intention is paved with good deeds."

107. *GSM*, 345.

108. *GSM*, 345.

109. *GSM*, 317.

110. *GSM*, 357.

111. *GSM*, 385.

112. *MNA*, 250.

113. *GSM*, 385–86.

114. *MNA*, 250.

115. *MNA*, 249.

116. *GSM*, 400.

117. *MNA,* 250.

118. *MG*, 278. See also *IF*, 146, repeated in *IE*, 160: "The ultimate concern of the Jew is not personal salvation but universal redemption."

119. *GSM*, 357.

120. *MQG*, 151.

121. *EL*, 72; see also *IE*, 159.

122. *IE,* 158–59.

123. *IF*, 238.

124. *MQG*, 151.
125. *MNA*, 243.
126. *PT*, 301.
127. *IE*, 145.

Chapter 4, pages 74–92

1. *MG*, 244. See also *MG*, 405: "As far as I can judge, and I try to judge God's will from history, it seems to be the will of God that there be more than one religion. . . . Yes, I think it is the will of God that there should be religious pluralism."

2. *MNA*, 119.

3. *MG*, 243.

4. *MNA*, 123.

5. Abraham Joshua Heschel, in "Two Conversations with Abraham Joshua Heschel," part 2, a transcript of "The Eternal Light" program, presented by the National Broadcasting Company (March 26, 1972), 9. Heschel was interviewed by Wolfe Kelman, executive vice president of The Rabbinical Assembly.

6. *MNA*, 145.

7. *MG*, 243.

8. *MG*, 243.

9. *GSM*, 415. On the same page, Heschel writes: "What is an idol? A thing, a force, a person, a group, an institution or an ideal, regarded as supreme. God alone is supreme."

10. *GSM*, 217.

11. *GSM*, 401; *MG*, 245.

12. *MNA*, 174.

13. *IF*, 181.

14. *MG*, 195, 194.

15. *MG*, 247.

16. *MG*, 245.

17. *MNA*, 111, 112.

18. *IF*, 95; *MNA*, 109.

19. *MNA*, 111.

20. *MNA*, 113.

21. *MNA*, 114.

22. *MNA*, 114.

23. *MNA*, 68.

24. *GSM*, 125.

25. *MNA*, 226.

26. *WM*, 71.

27. *GSM*, 162.

28. *MNA*, 117.

29. The term "panentheism" is used variously by various authors, as is evident, e.g., in the book *In Whom We Live and Move and Have Our Being: Panentheistic Reflections on God's Presence in a Scientific World*, eds. Philip Clayton and Arthur Peacocke (Grand Rapids, MI: William B. Eerdmans, 2004), but since the term is usually understood to mean, in the words the *Oxford Dictionary of the Christian Church*, "the belief that the

Being of God includes and penetrates the whole universe, so that every part of it exists in Him," I find it problematic to refer to Heschel's theology as panentheistic without dissociating it from the common sense of the term.

30. *MNA*, 112.

31. *MNA*, 121.

32. *MNA*, 100.

33. *IF*, 92.

34. *GSM*, 375, 376.

35. *GSM*, 238, 376.

36. *S*, 110; repeated in *GSM*, 94.

37. See my article "Heschel's Monotheism vis-à-vis Pantheism and Panentheism," *Studies in Christian-Jewish Relations* (2007; http://escholarship.bc.edu/scjr/vol2/iss2/): 26–33, in which I respond to several scholars who refer to Heschel's theology as panentheistic.

38. *MNA*, 78.

39. *MNA*, 148; *MQG*, 121; *GSM*, 97.

40. *MNA*, 240.

41. *WM*, 93.

42. *GSM*, 90.

43. *MNA*, 94, 226.

44. *MG*, 398.

45. *IE*, 212.

46. Discussions about "anonymous Christianity" and "anonymous Christians" are found in many of Rahner's writings. See especially the essays "Anonymous Christians," in Karl Rahner, *Theological Investigations*, vol. 6, trans. Karl-H. and Boniface Kruger (London: Darton, Longman & Todd; Baltimore: Helicon Press, 1969), 390–98; and "Anonymous Christianity and the Missionary Task of the Church," in Karl Rahner, *Theological Investigations*, vol. 12, trans. David Bourke (London: Darton, Longman & Todd; New York: Seabury Press, 1974), 161–78.

47. Karl Rahner, *Theological Investigations*, vol. 5, trans. Karl-H. Kruger (London: Darton, Longman & Todd; Baltimore: Helicon Press, 1966), 118.

48. See note 93 below where, in response to a critique of my position advanced in a previous publication, I discuss this issue further.

49. Harold Kasimow, "The Jewish Tradition and the Bhagavadgita," *Journal of Dharma* (July–September, 1983): 298. Along with the essays and book cited below in note 98, Kasimow's many contributions to the understanding of Heschel's theology, particularly of Heschel's approach to religious diversity, include his book *Divine-Human Encounter: A Study of Abraham Joshua Heschel* (Washington DC: University Press of America, 1979); his editing of a special issue of *Shofar: An Interdisciplinary Journal of Jewish Studies* (Fall 2007) titled *A Jewish Life: Abraham Joshua Heschel—A Centenary Tribute*; and his essays "Abraham Joshua Heschel and Interreligious Dialogue," *Journal of Ecumenical Studies* (Summer 1981): 423–34, and "Abraham Joshua Heschel and Swami Vivekananda, *Shofar: An Interdisciplinary Journal of Jewish Studies* (Spring 1999): 51–57. The latter is reprinted in Kasimow's book *The Search Will Make You Free: A Jewish Dialogue with World Religions* (Kraków, Poland: Wydawnictwo WAM, 2006), 195–204.

50. *GSM*, 15.

51. *MG*, 243.

52. *MG*, 244–45.

53. *MG*, 247.

54. *MG*, 246.

55. *IF*, 180.

56. *MG*, 238.

57. *IF*, 164.

58. *MG*, 244; see also *IF*, 182: "God's voice speaks in many languages, communicating itself in a diversity of intuitions."

59. *MG*, 245; see also *IF*, 182: "The word of God never comes to an end. No word is God's last word."

60. Abraham Joshua Heschel, in "Two Conversations with Abraham Joshua Heschel," part 1, a transcript of "The Eternal Light" program, presented by the National Broadcasting Company (March 17, 1972), 8.

61. *MG*, 244.

62. *MG*, 248.

63. *MG*, 249.

64. *MNA*, 108.

65. *MNA*, 112.

66. *GSM*, 323.

67. *IE*, 186.

68. *IE*, 212.

69. *GSM*, 7; repeated in *IF*, 117–18.

70. *GSM*, 154.

71. *GSM*, 154.

72. *MNA*, 166.

73. Heschel sometimes uses the terms "belief" and "faith" interchangeably, but when he does, "belief" carries the connotations ascribed to "faith" (trust, fidelity, etc.); with reference to God, it is meant to express the idea of believing in God, not simply believing that God exists or that a proposition about God is true.

74. *MNA*, 166.

75. *GSM*, 34; repeated in italics, *GSM*, 58.

76. *GSM*, 330, 331.

77. *MG*, 270.

78. *MNA*, 87; repeated in *GSM*, 138.

79. *MNA*, 167.

80. *MNA*, 169; repeated in *IF*, 121.

81. *MNA*, 168; *GSM*, 103.

82. *IF*, 177.

83. *GSM*, 331.

84. *P*, 221.

85. *MNA*, 98.

86. *MG*, 239.

87. *MNA*, 170.

88. *MNA*, 170.

89. *MG*, 236.

90. *MG*, 240.

91. *MNA*, 163–64.

92. *MNA*, 98–99.

93. *MG*, 244; see also *MNA*, 164. In his probing and insightful article "No Religion Is an Island: Following the Trail Blazer," *Shofar: An Interdisciplinary Journal of Jewish Studies* (Fall 2007): 72–111, Alon Goshen-Gottstein says about this same quotation: "This is a stunning passage. It sidesteps intention and the conscious awareness of believers and supplants them with a higher perspective that really belongs to God alone, through which they are recognized as worshipping God, even though they may not be aware of it" (94). Then, as a footnote to that comment, he says in response to my previously making a claim that I reiterate earlier in this chapter: "Merkle . . . claims that Heschel does not develop a Jewish notion analogous to Rahner's 'anonymous Christianity.' Some such similar anonymity must be acknowledged, however, as a means of relating the worship of other gods to the one true God" (94). Goshen-Gottstein is here responding to my claim made in my essay "Heschel's Attitude toward Religious Pluralism," in *No Religion Is an Island: Abraham Joshua Heschel and Interreligious Dialogue*, eds. Harold Kasimow and Byron L. Sherwin (Maryknoll, NY: Orbis Books, 1991), 99. As suggested earlier in this chapter, I agree that Heschel implies that there are what might be called "anonymous monotheists," that he believes that people who are not explicitly monotheists may none-theless have an implied experience of and responsiveness to God. But I still maintain that Heschel does not suggest that these implicit monotheists are somehow anonymous Jews; he does not presume that people either have to be Jewish or somehow related to Judaism, even if only implicitly, in order to live in accord with God.

94. See *MNA*, 33.

95. *IF*, 54.

96. *IF*, 54.

97. *MG*, 247.

98. Harold Kasimow, "Heschel's View of Religious Diversity," *Studies in Christian-Jewish Relations* (2007; http://escholarship.bc.edu/scjr/vol2/iss2/): 22. See also Harold Kasimow, "Heschel's Prophetic Vision of Religious Pluralism," in *No Religion Is an Island: Abraham Joshua Heschel and Interreligious Dialogue*, eds. Harold Kasimow and Byron L. Sherwin (Maryknoll, NY: Orbis Books, 1991), 88: "What was critical for Heschel was not *what* religion an individual belonged to, but *how* human he or she really was; what is most significant is not the tradition the individual follows but how pious the individual is in life."

99. *IF*, 86.

100. *IF*, 87, 98–99, 99.

101. *IF*, 180.

BIBLIOGRAPHY

For the most complete list of writings by and about Heschel up to 1975, see Fritz A. Rothschild's bibliography in the revised edition of *Between God and Man: An Interpretation of Judaism from the Writings of Abraham J. Heschel*. For an extensive bibliography of Heschel's writings, including books and essays published posthumously through 2005, as well as many secondary sources, see the bibliography (under the heading "References") in Edward K. Kaplan's *Spiritual Radical: Abraham Joshua Heschel in America*. There are also extensive bibliographies in Harold Kasimow and Byron Sherwin's *No Religion Is an Island: Abraham Joshua Heschel and Interreligious Dialogue* and in my *The Genesis of Faith: The Depth Theology of Abraham Joshua Heschel*.

This bibliography does not contain a section devoted to articles by Heschel because all but one of the articles quoted in this book have been republished in the more easily accessible anthologies that contain references to where the articles were originally published. I trust the references in my endnotes to the anthologies rather than to the many journals from which they are drawn are more helpful to most readers.

Selected Books by Abraham Joshua Heschel
(listed chronologically by category)

Books Written in English

The Quest for Certainty in Saadia's Philosophy. New York: Philip Feldheim, 1944.
The Earth Is the Lord's: The Inner Life of the Jew in East Europe. New York: Henry Shuman, 1950.
Man Is Not Alone: A Philosophy of Religion. New York: Farrar, Straus, and Young; Philadelphia: Jewish Publication Society of America, 1951.
The Sabbath: Its Meaning for Modern Man. New York: Farrar, Straus, and Young, 1951.
Man's Quest for God: Studies in Prayer and Symbolism. New York: Charles Scribner's Sons, 1954.

God in Search of Man: A Philosophy of Judaism. New York: Farrar, Straus, and Cudahy; Philadelphia: Jewish Publication Society of America, 1955.

The Prophets. New York: Harper and Row; Philadelphia: Jewish Publication Society of America, 1962.

Who Is Man? Stanford, CA: Stanford University Press, 1965.

Israel: An Echo of Eternity. New York: Farrar, Straus, and Giroux, 1969.

A Passion for Truth. New York: Farrar, Straus, and Giroux, 1973.

Books Translated into English

Maimonides: A Biography. Translated by Joachim Neugroschel. New York: Farrar, Straus, and Giroux, 1982. Translation of *Maimonides: Eine Biographie* (German). Berlin: Erich Reiss Verlag, 1935.

The Ineffable Name of God: Man. Poems. Translated by Morton Leifman. New York and London: Continuum, 2005. Translation of *Der Shem Hameforash: Mentsh* (Yiddish). Warsaw: Farlag Indzl, 1933.

Heavenly Torah As Refracted through the Generations. Edited and translated by Gordon Tucker, with Leonard Levin. New York and London: Continuum, 2005. Translation of *Torah min Hashamayim Ba-Aspaklariah shel Hadorot* (Hebrew). 3 vols. Vols. 1 and 2, London and New York: Soncino Press, 1962, 1965; Vol. 3, New York and Jerusalem: Jewish Theological Seminary, 1990.

Anthologies in English

Between God and Man: An Interpretation of Judaism from the Writings of Abraham J. Heschel. Edited by Fritz A. Rothschild. New York: Free Press, 1959. Revised introduction and bibliography, 1975.

The Insecurity of Freedom: Essays on Human Existence. New York: Farrar, Straus, and Giroux, 1966.

Moral Grandeur and Spiritual Audacity. Edited by Susannah Heschel. New York: Farrar, Straus, and Giroux, 1996.

Selected Books about Abraham Joshua Heschel

Friedman, Maurice. *You Are My Witnesses: Abraham Heschel and Elie Wiesel.* New York: Farrar, Straus, and Giroux, 1987.

Kaplan, Edward K. *Holiness in Words: Abraham Joshua Heschel's Poetics of Piety.* Albany, NY: State University of New York Press, 1996.

———. *Spiritual Radical: Abraham Joshua Heschel in America.* New Haven and London: Yale University Press, 2007.

——— and Samuel H. Dresner. *Abraham Joshua Heschel: Prophetic Witness.* New Haven and London: Yale University Press, 1998.

Kasimow, Harold. *Divine-Human Encounter: A Study of Abraham Joshua Heschel.* Washington, DC: University Press of America, 1979.

———— and Byron L. Sherwin, eds. *No Religion Is an Island: Abraham Joshua Heschel and Interreligious Dialogue.* Maryknoll, NY: Orbis Books, 1991.

Merkle, John C., ed. *Abraham Joshua Heschel: Exploring His Life and Thought.* New York and London: Macmillan, 1985.

————. *The Genesis of Faith: The Depth Theology of Abraham Joshua Heschel.* New York and London: Macmillan, 1985.

Moore, Donald. *The Human and the Holy: The Spirituality of A. J. Heschel.* New York: Fordham University Press, 1989.

Perlman, Lawrence. *Abraham Heschel's Idea of Revelation.* Atlanta: Scholars Press, 1989.

Sherman, Franklin. *The Promise of Heschel.* The Promise of Theology Series. Philadelphia and New York: J. B . Lippincott, 1970.

Sherwin, Byron L. *Abraham Joshua Heschel.* Markers of Contemporary Theology Series. Atlanta: John Knox Press, 1979.

Other Works Cited

Bennett, John C. "Agent of God's Compassion." *America* 128, no. 9 (March 10, 1973): 205–6.

Brown, Robert McAfee. "Abraham Heschel: A Passion for Sincerity." *Christianity and Crisis* 33, no. 21 (December 10, 1973): 256–59.

————. "Heschel's Social Ethics." In *Abraham Joshua Heschel: Exploring His Life and Thought*, edited by John C. Merkle, 123–41. New York and London: Macmillan, 1985.

Cherbonnier, Edmond La B. "Heschel as a Religious Thinker." *Conservative Judaism* 23, no.1 (Fall 1968): 25–39.

Clayton, Philip, and Arthur Peacocke, eds. *In Whom We Live and Move and Have Our Being: Panentheistic Reflections on God's Presence in a Scientific World.* Grand Rapids, MI: Eerdmans, 2004.

"Conversation with Martin Luther King." *Conservative Judaism* 22, no. 3 (Spring 1968): 1–19.

Davies, W. D. "Conscience, Scholar, Witness." *America* 128, no. 9 (March 10, 1973): 213–15.

Dresner, Samuel H. "Introduction: Heschel as a Hasidic Scholar." In Abraham J. Heschel, *The Circle of the Baal Shem Tov: Studies in Hasidism*, edited by Samuel H. Dresner, vii–xlv. Chicago and London: University of Chicago Press, 1985.

Even-Chen, Alexander. "God's Omnipotence and Presence in Abraham Joshua Heschel's Philosophy." *Shofar: An Interdisciplinary Journal of Jewish Studies* 26, no. 1 (Fall 2007): 41–71.

Goshen-Gottstein, Alon. "No Religion Is an Island: Following the Trail Blazer." *Shofar: An Interdisciplinary Journal of Jewish Studies* 26, no. 1 (Fall 2007): 72–111.

Heschel, Abraham J. "The Moral Outrage of Vietnam." In *Vietnam: Crisis of Conscience*, edited by Robert McAfee Brown, Abraham J. Heschel, and Michael Novak, 48–61. New York: Herder and Herder, 1967.

Heschel, Susannah. "Introduction." In Abraham J. Heschel, *Moral Grandeur and Spiritual Audacity*, edited by Susannah Heschel, vii–xxx. New York: Farrar, Straus, and Giroux, 1996.

Kaplan, Edward K. "Form and Content in Abraham J. Heschel's Poetic Style." *Central Conference of American Rabbis Journal* 18, no. 2 (April 1971): 28–39.

Kasimow, Harold, ed. *A Jewish Life: Abraham Joshua Heschel—A Centenary Tribute*. Special issue of *Shofar: An Interdisciplinary Journal of Jewish Studies* 26, no. 1 (Fall 2007).

———. "Abraham Joshua Heschel and Interreligious Dialogue." *Journal of Ecumenical Studies* 18, no. 3 (Summer 1981): 423–34.

———. "Abraham Joshua Heschel and Swami Vivekananda." *Shofar: An Interdisciplinary Journal of Jewish Studies* 17, no. 3 (Spring 1999): 51–57.

———. "Heschel's Prophetic Vision of Religious Pluralism." In *No Religion Is an Island: Abraham Joshua Heschel and Interreligious Dialogue*, edited by Harold Kasimow and Byron L. Sherwin, 79–96. Maryknoll, NY: Orbis Books, 1991.

———. "Heschel's View of Religious Diversity." *Studies in Christian-Jewish Relations* 2, no. 2 (2007): 19–25. http://escholarship.bc.edu/scjr/vol2/iss2/.

———. "The Jewish Tradition and the Bhagavadgita." *Journal of Dharma* 8, no. 3 (July–September, 1983): 296–310.

———. *The Search Will Make You Free: A Jewish Dialogue with World Religions*. Kraków, Poland: Wydawnictwo WAM, 2006.

Kimelman, Reuven. "Abraham Joshua Heschel (1907-1972)." *Response: A Contemporary Jewish Review* 6, no. 4 (Winter 1972–73): 15–22.

Merkle, John C. "Heschel's Attitude toward Religious Pluralism." In *No Religion Is an Island: Abraham Joshua Heschel and Interreligious Dialogue*, edited by Harold Kasimow and Byron L. Sherwin, 97–109. Maryknoll, NY: Orbis Books, 1991.

———. "Heschel's Monotheism vis-à-vis Pantheism and Panentheism." *Studies in Christian-Jewish Relations* 2, no. 2 (2007): 26–33. http://escholarship.bc.edu/scjr/vol2/iss2/.

———. "Heschel's Theology of Divine Pathos." In *Abraham Joshua Heschel: Exploring His Life and Thought*, edited by John C. Merkle, 66–83. New York and London: Macmillan, 1985.

Otto, Rudolf. *The Idea of the Holy*, translated by John W. Harvey. Oxford and New York: Oxford University Press, 1958.

Rahner, Karl. *Theological Investigations*. Vol. 5, translated by Karl-H. Kruger. London: Darton, Longman and Todd; Baltimore: Helicon Press, 1966.

———. *Theological Investigations*. Vol. 6, translated by Karl-H. and Boniface Kruger. London: Darton, Longman and Todd; Baltimore: Helicon Press, 1969.

———. *Theological Investigations*. Vol. 12, translated by David Bourke. London: Darton, Longman and Todd; New York: Seabury Press, 1974.

Rothschild, Fritz A. "Abraham Joshua Heschel (1907–1972): Theologian and Scholar." *American Jewish Yearbook* 74 (1973): 533–44.

———. "Architect and Herald of a New Theology." *America* 128, no. 9 (March 10, 1973): 210–12.

———. "Introduction." In *Between God and Man: An Interpretation of Judaism from the Writings of Abraham J. Heschel*, edited by Fritz A. Rothschild, 7–32. New York: Free Press, 1959. Revised introduction and bibliography, 1975.

———. "Varieties of Heschelian Thought." In *Abraham Joshua Heschel: Exploring His Life and Thought*, edited by John C. Merkle, 87–102. New York and London: Macmillan, 1985.

Sanders, J. A. "An Apostle to the Gentiles." *Conservative Judaism* 28, no. 1 (Fall 1973): 61–63.

Sherwin, Byron. "Abraham Joshua Heschel." *The Torch* (Spring 1969): 5–8.

Spiro, Jack D. "Rabbi Abraham Joshua Heschel: An Appreciation." *Religious Education* 68, no. 2 (March–April 1973): 218–25.

Starkman, Moshe. "Abraham Joshua Heschel: The Jewish Writer and Thinker." *Conservative Judaism* 28, no. 1 (Fall 1973): 75–77.

Teshima, Jacob Y. "My Memory of Professor Abraham Joshua Heschel." *Conservative Judaism* 28, no. 1 (Fall 1973): 78–80.

Whitehead, Alfred North. *Science and the Modern World*. New York: Macmillan, 1926.

———. *Process and Reality: An Essay in Cosmology*. New York: Macmillan, 1929.

INDEX

Abravanel, Don Isaac, 6
action, ethical / good deeds (*see also*
   mitsvah / mitsvot)
   delighting in, 71–72
   faith and, 69–71, 73
   immanence of God in, 70
   kavanah and, 69–71
   as primary way of serving God,
     68–69
   redemption through, 72–73, 86
   worship and, 68–69, 92
agada (Jewish lore), 51–52
anonymous Christianity / anonymous Christians, 81–82, 107n46,
   109n93
Aquinas, Thomas, 46
Aristotle / Aristotelian, 46, 95n12,
   102n78
awe
   as antithesis of fear, 58
   as beginning of wisdom, 59
   as prerequisite and aspect of
     worship, 57, 59
   as prerequisite of ethical living, 58
   as response to mystery and God,
     57–58

Baal Shem Tov (Israel ben Eliezer),
   1–2, 9, 67
being
   creation of, 30–31
   in and beyond all beings, 19–20, 80

   mystery of, 16, 17, 30
   sacredness of all, 81
   static vs. dynamic concepts of,
     44–45
   transcendent concern or care for,
     28, 31
beliefs about God (*see also* doctrines
   about God, faith in God), 27–28,
   37–38, 87–88
Bennett, John C., 10
Bible (*see also* Torah)
   authorship of, 42–43
   and faith in God, 48
   God's presence in, 41–42
   idea of divine pathos in, 43–48
   as *midrash*, 49
   rabbinic interpretation of, 49–50
   responsiveness to, 40–41
   revelation and, 40–54
blasphemy, 5, 92
Brown, Robert McAfee, 1, 10, 12
Buber, Martin, 6

Christianity / Christians, 11–12,
   81–82, 85–86, 89–90
chosen people, 84–85
compassion, human (*see also* God,
   compassion of)
   as divine gift, 26–27
   for God, 73
   worship and, 68–69, 92
conscience, 25–26